THOMAS DUNCKERLEY

A Remarkable Freemason

Figure 1
Portrait of Thomas Dunckerley by Thomas Beach 1787

THOMAS DUNCKERLEY

A Remarkable Freemason

Ron Chudley

LONDON
LEWIS MASONIC

© 1982 R. Chudley

Published by LEWIS MASONIC
Terminal House, Shepperton TW17 8AS, Middlesex
Members of IAN ALLAN GROUP

ISBN 0 85318 129 2

First published 1982

British Library Cataloguing in Publication Data
Chudley, Ron
   Thomas Dunckerley
   1. Dunckerley, Thomas   2. Freemasons—
   Biography
   I. Title
   366'.1'0924   HS596.A6/

Made and printed in Great Britain by The Garden City Press Limited,
Letchworth, Hertfordshire SG6 1JS

Contents

Illustrations

Foreword

It is always refreshing to turn to the early incidents of our history and learn from the acts of Great Men who have gone to their account.

I am sure all who are privileged to read this book will be most grateful to W Bro C. R. T. Chudley for searching out all the details of this amazing and tenacious Brother.

Thomas Dunckerley seems to have run away from school at an early age and joined the Navy as a 'Powder Monkey' and eventually became a Master Gunner.

In this capacity he took part in the Siege of Quebec on 18 August 1759 when General James Wolfe defeated Montcalm.

During his life in the Navy he became a freemason and in spite of the very hard life in the Service his interest became intense.

Eventually his financial and other troubles were solved and he became dedicated to our Order.

I strongly recommend this book to every Brother of our Order in the hope it will give him pleasure and encouragement.

WalKneel

RW Bro W. A. Kneel
Provincial Grand Master of Devonshire

Acknowledgements for the Illustrations

The frontispiece portrait of Dunckerley and the engraving taken from this portrait (fig 20) is reproduced by permission of Loyal Lodge No 251, Barnstaple. The certificate (fig 2) is reproduced with permission of the Public Records Office, Ontario, Canada. The letter (fig 4) is in the Grand Lodge of Canada archives and reproduced with their permission. The Muster lists for HMS *Vanguard* and *Prince* (figs 6 and 7) are reproduced by courtesy of the Public Record Office, Kew. The letter (fig 9) is reproduced with permission of the Norman Masonic Museum and Library, Bath. Various letters written by Dunckerley (figs 11 to 16 inclusive and figs 25 and 26) are all the property of the Coombe Library and are reproduced by permission of Cornubian Lodge No 450, Hayle, Cornwall. The engraving by West (fig 21) is reproduced with permission of Lodge of Amity No 137 and the title page from *The Light & Truth of Masonry* (fig 23) is reproduced by permission of the Board of General Purposes. The Certificate (fig 3) is reproduced with permission of the Board of General Purposes, United Grand Lodge of England. The minute in cypher (fig 5) is copied by the author from *History of the Phoenix Lodge and Chapter of Friendship No 257* published by Alexander Howell in 1894, the code and translation having been added. The artist's impression of HMS *Vanguard* (fig 8) is taken from a painting by A. F. Calvert for his book *The Grand Lodge of England 1717–1917*. The hymn reproduced as fig 10 has words by Bishop W. Walsham How and was set to music by R. Vaughan Williams in 1872. Now adopted by many Knights Templar Preceptories. The Arms and Seals (figs 17 and 18) are taken from documents held by the United Grand Lodge of England, Cornubian Lodge No 450, Hayle and the Transactions of Quatuor Coronati Lodge, with whose permission they are reproduced. The portrait of King George II (fig 19) is taken from *Thomas Dunckerley* by Henry Sadler. The portrait of Dunckerley (fig 22) is taken from *Freemasonry in Bristol* by Powell and Littleton. The song (fig 24) is taken from an 18th-century edition of The *Freemasons' Magazine*.

1

A Frightening Secret

WITH A DIGNITY that defied her cumbersome bulk, His Majesty's
Ship *Vanguard* on 7 March 1760 eased her way from the shelter
of Spithead into the deep water east of the Isle of Wight. Then
with the main brace set, she headed down the English Channel
towards the vast expanse of the North Atlantic Ocean.

Her mission was urgent and Captain Robert Swanton had no
cause to remind his crew of the importance of a speedy return to
the St Lawrence River and the scene of one of the earliest and
most successful combined operations of the armed services in
the country's history.

Seventy guns lined the scrubbed decks of the wooden man-
o'-war, guns which had recently roared vengeance against the
French to force them to return Quebec to King George II.

In charge of the guns and those who manned them was
Thomas Dunckerley who was now returning to Canada not only
as the Master Gunner of *Vanguard* but also as the first official
emissary for freemasonry, for securely locked in the sea chest in
the cramped confines of his quarters was a document from the
Grand Lodge in London.

This document empowered Brother Thomas Dunckerley 'to
inspect the Craft wherever he might go'.

He had also a second document. It was a warrant dated 16
January 1760 and numbered 254, 'to hold a Lodge and make
Masons on board HMS *Vanguard*'.

For Dunckerley, who had been initiated just six years before,
it was virtually the start of a career which was to make him
pre-eminent among freemasons for all time and which was to
play a forceful part in making freemasonry the efficient and

1

organised institution it is today.

The aim of this book is to present the story of an intriguing and incredible man who, as the hero, would place a novel among the ranks of the best-sellers.

But the story of Thomas Dunckerley is not fiction. It is that of a boy from a fatherless home who, at the age of ten, ran away and sailed before the mast to engage the King's enemies.

It is the story of a man who, through unfortunate circumstances, was forced to flee the country 'fearful of being arrested' as a debtor. Friends who embraced the opportunity to practice that virtue which freemasons profess to admire, came to his assistance and he returned home to Plymouth to settle his debts.

Above all, it is the story of a freemason who rose to be the head of masons in eight counties thus becoming the patriarch of the present long line of Provincial Grand Masters.

He became the Grand Superintendent of 18 Royal Arch Provinces and as the Grand Master of Knights Templar he called on them to be ready to take up arms to ward off a threatened invasion.

As the prow of *Vanguard* sliced through the uneasy waters of the Atlantic Dunckerley must have had one predominant thought. It was the frightening secret of his birth which even his wife, at home in Plymouth, knew nothing.

He had just received information that he, a Gunner in the Royal Navy, was the illegitimate son of the reigning monarch, King George II of England.

2

AN UNHAPPY EVENT

THOMAS DUNCKERLEY WAS born on 23 October 1724 either in an apartment at the original Somerset House in London or in a house at Richmond where there were many royal residences. Unfortunately churches where the birth would have been registered have, with their records, been destroyed by the ravages of time and war.

The baby was delivered by the midwife to the Royal Family but his birth was anticipated with little joy by his mother while her husband regarded her and the baby with sheer contempt and disdain. At the time there was nothing about the unhappy events which could be regarded as romantic.

The dramatic manner in which Dunckerley received the news of his parentage, 36 years after his birth, is described in a document in his own handwriting. The contents of this document were published in the *Freemasons' Magazine* in February 1796, three months after his death, and later in the *Gentlemans' Magazine*.

It was introduced with these words: 'Further Particulars of the Late Thoms Dunckerley, Es., Communicated in his own handwriting by his Executors which fully contradict the many idle stories that have for some time been in circulation respecting him.'

The document read.

January 9, 1760, soon after my return from the siege of Quebec, I received an account of my mother's death; and having obtained permission from my captain to be absent from duty I went to London and attended her funeral.

3

Among the very few I invited to the ceremony was Mrs. Pinkney, who had been many years a neighbour to my mother in Somerset-house. On our return from the burial, she desired I would call on her the next day and not bring my wife with me having something of consequence to tell me. I waited on her accordingly; and the following is the substance of what she related to me, as I took it in writing:-

'Mary Dunckerley being dangerously ill with the gout in her stomach (January 2, 1760), and believing it will be her death, is desirous, at the request of her friend, Mrs. Pinkney, that the following account may be made known to her son in the most secret manner, and to none but him.

'At the latter end of November 1723, Mr. Dunckerley went to Chatsworth, in Derbyshire, on some business for the Duke of Devonshire, and did not return till the May following. At Christmas I went to see Mrs. Meeking at Lady Ranelagh's. Mr. L-----y happened to come there, and paid me the greatest respect and hinted that I stood in my own light, or I might be the happiest woman in England. I knew his meaning, but made no reply, and went back to Somerset-house the next day. A fortnight after, I had an invitation to Lady Ranelagh's, and her coach was sent for me. I was surprised to find Mr. L-----y there again. He handed me from the coach to the parlour; where, to my future unhappiness, I found the Prince of Wales, whom I had too well known before my unhappy marriage. At his request (for I could deny him nothing) I stayed several days during which time he made me five visits, and on Candlemas day I went home.

'Soon after I found myself sick and breeding, and was resolved to make an end to my life. I was taken very ill. Lady Stanley came to see me; but I could not let her know my disorder. Mrs. Meeking came to see me; and I told her the consequence of what had happened. The next day she came and brought me bank bills for £50 inclosed in a cover from Mr. Lumley acquainting me that it was by the Prince's command.

'She said Lady Ranelagh was coming to see me; in less than an hour her ladyship came; they advised me to go in the country, and said a house was taken for me at Richmond; but I was obstinate, and said I would not go out of the house until I was brough to-bed. I desired that they would never let the Prince of Wales or Mr. L-----y know that I was with child; and I never found they did. Dr. Mead attended me. He ordered me to be bled, and in two days I could sit up.

'Mr. Dunckerley came from Chatsworth in May, and seemed not displeased to find me with child. I disdained to deceive him; and told him what had happened. He commanded my conduct with so much joy, that I could not help despising his meanness; and his barbarous behaviour to me in the last month of my time was what I always resented, when he threw a cat in my face, and swore that he would mark the bastard. Our separation soon followed after my delivery; and he kept the secret on his own account; for he had two places and considerable advantages, as the price of my folly.

'My son might have been known to his royal father, and I might have lived in an elegant manner as Mrs. H. and Miss B.; but my dear mother reclaimed me from so criminal a passion and dread of public shame prevented my making it known.'

This is what Mrs. Pinkney assured me was my mother's declaration on her death-bed; for she departed this life five days after. She also told me that my grandmother Bolness, Mrs. Cannon, a midwife, and herself were present at my birth, October 23, 1724; that my mother then declared the Prince of Wales was my father; and that my grandmother and mother requested it might be kept a secret.

Mrs. Pinkney also informed me that my mother was a physician's daughter, and lived with Mrs. W. when the Prince of Wales debauched her; but that Mrs. W. discovered what had happened, and had her married to Mr Dunckerley, who was then attending the Duke of Devonshire, on a visit to Sir R.W. . . . . . at Houghton.

It is fortunate that surviving the ravages of time are a few magazines which contain the document which tells the remarkable story of events which led to the birth of one of the greatest of all freemasons. Read the document again and you will have revealed a sad story of intrigue and pathos.

As I see it (and filling in the spaces) it is the story of an attractive young woman named Mary, the daughter of a Dr and Mrs Bolness, who took an appointment with Mrs Walpole, the wife of Robert Walpole, the first English Prime Minister, who was knighted in 1725.

A frequent visitor to the Walpole ancestral and stately home at Houghton was the Prince of Wales, a man in his late thirties. He found Mary irresistible and, flattered by the ardent attentions of such an important person, Mary 'refused him nothing';

she became his mistress.

The affair caused Mrs Walpole considerable concern. She had probably seen it all before and she knew there could be no satisfactory outcome for the young woman for whom she felt some responsibility.

Another frequent visitor to Houghton was the Duke of Devonshire. He was attended by a man named Dunckerley and in him Mrs Walpole saw a solution. She arranged a marriage between Dunckerley and Mary. It was certainly not a love match for Mary herself refers to it as 'my unhappy marriage'. It was either a marriage of convenience to cover any eventuality or one arranged in the hope that any illicit affair would end.

Mary left Houghton to live with her husband in Somerset House, a property owned by the Court, but it was not long before Mr Dunckerley had once more to go away with the Duke of Devonshire, this time to Chatsworth which had been designed by the famous architect William Talman in 1687 for the Duke's father.

In the atmosphere and beauty, the house rivalled Houghton, and it was whilst Mr Dunckerley was there, enjoying all the then ultra-modern amenities, including such refinements as water closets, that the Prince of Wales once again directed his attention to Mary.

To renew the contract he sent Charles Lumley, who besides being a Colonel in the Grenadier Guards, held the more pertinent appointment of Groom to the Bed Chamber!

Also into the story came Lady Ranelagh, the widowed daughter of the Earl of Salisbury, who invited Mary to visit her. It was at her house that the Prince awaited.

When she found she was pregnant, Mary, in desperation, shame and remorse, tried to commit suicide, and became desperately ill. The Prince sent her £50, a considerable sum of money in those days, and to their credit Lady Stanley, wife of Sir John Stanley, from Dublin, who held various government posts, and her friend Lady Ranelagh, visited Mary during her illness. The baby was delivered by Mrs Cannon, midwife to the Royal household.

Mary's mother persuaded her from the impulse to name the

baby's father in the hope of living 'in as elegant a manner' as Mrs
Howard, afterwards Lady Suffolk, and Mary Bellenden, who
were maids of honour to the Princess of Wales.

It would have been too much for Mr Dunckerley to be pleased
when he learned the truth about the baby, but his violent
behaviour was beyond excess. His departure from the home was
probably not regretted. He had been given 'two places and
considerable advantages' to buy his silence.

In some ways it was an old, old story of the girl paying the
penalty, but what mental torture Mary must have suffered. She
died believing that few knew the truth. How mistaken she must
have been for there were far too many people involved. Mary
would have kept the knowledge to herself had not Mrs Pinkney
prevailed on her to make a statement.

3

THE YOUNG RUNAWAY

FOR INFORMATION ON Thomas Dunckerley's childhood we can
turn only to an article which was published during his lifetime. It
appeared in the *Freemasons' Magazine* in October 1793 and was
written by Brother T. White, a teacher at Colchester University
who was described by the proprietors of the magazine as a
valued contributor.

As he was the Provincial Grand Junior Warden of Essex when
Dunckerley was the Provincial Grand Master it can be assumed
that the details came from Dunckerley and are authentic. White
wrote

... Honestas et Fortitude was a motto which he (Dunckerley) took
at 10 years of age, when a thirst for glory and a desire to engage in

the bustle of the world induced him to leave school abruptly and
enter the Royal Navy . . .

Thomas had probably been sent away from his mother and the
fatherless home to a boarding school where discipline was harsh
and he was just one of a bunch of unhappy, unwanted boys.

Dunckerley retired from the Navy in May 1767. White, in his
article, refers to '26 years constant service in the Navy' which
suggests that Dunckerley enlisted in 1741. He was then 16 years
of age.

He was ten, maybe nearly 11, when he ran away, and even in
the harsh years of the mid-seventeen hundreds a boy of that age
could not just enter the Navy without some formalities; com-
pleting these could well take 12 months. 'Boys' service' was
probably not taken into account when assessing constant service
and the reference to 26 years could have been a loose statement
making use of a round figure. In working along these lines there
seems to be some three or four years unaccounted for, doubtless
uninteresting childhood years long forgotten.

Soon after his death in 1795 a short article appeared in the
Gentleman's Magazine which circulated among the eighteenth-
century society. The article stated, '. . . his grandmother took
care of him till he was put apprentice to a barber. From this place
he ran away and got on board the ship of Sir John Norris, who
was just going abroad . . .'

In the anonymous article there are several proved inac-
curacies and it is not known what reliance can be placed on this
statement but employment by the barber could account for the
missing years. At this particular time the *Gentleman's Magazine*
was adopting an anti-masonic policy and in June 1794 printed
an anonymous article in which the writer made an insidious
attack on the Craft and accused it of being responsible for the
French Revolution.

4

MASTER OF PLYMOUTH LODGES

DUNCKERLEY WAS 29 years of age when he was initiated in a
lodge which met at the Three Tuns Tavern at Portsmouth.

What induced him to become a mason? To this date the sea
had virtually been his life, but it had brought him into contact
with freemasons in all parts of the world including the Earl of
Chesterfield and Royal Navy Captain Mark Robinson, two men
he held in high esteem.

When ships in which he served were at Portsmouth and fellow
crew members went ashore to lodge meetings his interest was
aroused. The Three Tuns Lodge had a membership comprising
naval and army officers and senior-non-commissioned officers
as well as local professional and successful tradesmen. Captain
Robinson had been a member since 1747 and faithfully served
the lodge after a brilliant naval career.

Another member was Captain Robert Roddam who became
Commander-in-Chief at the Nore and an Admiral of the Blue
and the White.

The date and place of his initiation is contained in a letter
written by Dunckerley so that it is beyond speculation and it is
certain that no one present on 10 January 1754 when he was
initiated, passed and raised, anticipated that the young, eager
and fervent schoolmaster from HMS *Tyger* would one day
become one of the greatest men in masonic history.

It was a Brother Dunckerley, full of enthusiasm for
freemasonry, who returned to his home in Plymouth which was
a hive of masonic activity with a strong service following. There
he joined the Pope's Head Tavern Lodge which was warranted
in 1748 and met in Pike Street (now Looe Street), Plymouth,

9

and also the Masons' Arms Tavern Lodge, warranted in 1734, which met in a room at Pembroke Street, Plymouth Dock, now known as Devonport.

This was the start of a career which would contribute to enhance the status of freemasonry to such an extent that the name of Thomas Dunckerley would be honoured not only in English-speaking countries but throughout the world.

In Plymouth he met more naval and military freemasons. The Pope's Head Tavern, not far from the spot on Plymouth Hoe where Sir Francis Drake played his historic game of bowls before defeating the Spanish Armada 200 years before, was a popular venue for the 'sea dogs' of England and Dunckerley must have been in his element, both as a mariner and a mason.

He was a man of strong faith and pleasing personality and on or during the week of St John's day in December 1756 he became the 'Right Worshipful Master' of both lodges, having first filled the warden's chairs. Masters were elected for six months and in both lodges Brother Dunckerley occupied the chair for two unbroken years.

As the lodges met twice monthly this must have involved a great deal of travel for in those days the rivers had not been bridged nor the swamps reclaimed so that to go by horseback or on foot from Devonport to the far side of Plymouth involved a long and slow detour along unlighted tracks into the countryside.

In the lodges there were no written rituals and ceremonies were by catechism or, in other words, by question and answer and depending on the Masters there must have been a great deal of variety in the workings of the individual lodges.

With his own definite ideas of the tenets of freemasonry, a precise mind and flair for words, Dunckerley began to regularise the ritual in his own lodges and enthusiasm eventually led him to additional degrees, many of which, rightly or wrongly, he is credited with writing.

With the enthusiasm in the lodges and the attraction of the new degrees, Plymouth gained a reputation as a centre for freemasonry and it was not long before a larger meeting room was needed.

This was opened on 28 April 1757 and for the occasion Dunckerley prepared an oration which he entitled *The Light and Truth of Masonry Explained.* It was published and sold for six pence and in 1793 was printed in the *Freemasons' Magazine.* It is given in full in a later chapter.

In 1755 an important development in the military prestige and defence of the country occurred. It was the formation of the First Plymouth Division of the Royal Marines and many of the officers and NCOs were known to Dunckerley as freemasons. It was an opportunity which could not be missed; he contacted these brethren and was instrumental in inducing them to apply for a warrant to form a new lodge and doubtless he had ambitions to be the first Master.

But it was a time of international tension and the beginning of colonising and empire building and many demands were being made on the Royal Navy and it was no surprise to Dunckerley when the call came for him temporarily to lay aside his local freemasonry.

His ship, *Vanguard*, in which he was the Master Gunner was being fitted out in Plymouth Dockyard and on 15 October 1757 she moved to an anchorage in St John's Lake, opposite Mutton Cove, to take on guns, ammunition and stores. Three weeks later she was anchored in Plymouth's famous Sound before sailing to join Admiral Boscawen's fleet in what is known now as the Western Approaches to assist in the blockade of the French ports. The following April she headed for the North American station.

It was five years before Dunckerley resumed his Plymouth freemasonry and by that time the Marine Lodge was formed and his name, therefore, does not appear on the original warrant. It names Samuel Simpson as Master, Andrew Allen as Senior Warden, William Brown as Junior Warden and Richard Hayes as the Secretary.

The most precious possession of the Marine Lodge – now Fortitude No 105 – is the original warrant which was one of the first issued under the English Constitution.

An indication of the respect gained by Dunckerley in Plymouth is that when he left to reside at Somerset House the brethren of the Masons' Arms Lodge presented him with a framed testimonial in 1768 recording his services to the Lodge. The certificate said that during two years Dunckerley was Master '. . . his masonic skill, knowledge and experience hath been manifested in the care he hath taken in governing, instructing and improving the said Lodge in the several degrees of E.A.: FC .. .. MM .. .. .. and RA .. ..'

The dots are of interest and importance and the wording gives proof of his zeal for the Royal Arch degree even before Grand Chapter issued warrants.

5

QUEBEC INSTALLATION

IN THE INTERVENING years before he was able to resume his masonic activities in Plymouth, Dunckerley sailed the Atlantic four times to and from Quebec. The famous battle of the Plains was fought on 13 September 1759 and two weeks later the British marched into Quebec.

Six of the British regiments which had assembled for the battle had lodges attached, five of them being constituted by warrants from the Grand Lodge of Ireland which issued no less than 51 military warrants in the 30 years to 1762. The sixth lodge was warranted by the Provincial Grand Lodge of Massachusetts.

Freemasonry was one of the few means of social communication and relaxation in this area of uncertain peace. There were a large number of military masons and the need for co-ordination of the lodges and ceremonies became obvious and soon after the surrender of Quebec a meeting of all the regional lodges was called. The meeting was attended by the masters and wardens of the following lodges.

No 192 attached to the 47th Regiment
No 218 attached to the 48th Regiment
Dispensation No 195 – Artillery
(The above all registered with the Grand Lodge of Ireland)

No 1 of Louisbourg warrant
No 245 attached to the 15th Regiment
Dispensation No 136-43rd Regiment

It is recorded that on 28 November 1759 they met,

> . . . in form at 6 o'clock in the Evening when it was Consulted and agreed upon, as there were so many Lodges in this Garrison, that one of the Brethren present of the Greatest Skill and Merrit should take upon him the Name of GRAND MASTER from the Authority of the above lodges untill such time as a favourable opportunity should offer for obtaining a proper Sanction from the Right Worshipful and Right Honourable the Grand Master of England and in Censequence thereof our True and faithful Brother Mr. John Price Guinett Lieutenant in his Majesty's 47th. Regiment was unanimously and to the Great satisfaction of the whole Fraternity assembled Proclaimed GRAND MASTER for the Ensuing year . . .

It has been suggested that Dunckerley was asked to obtain the sanction but any inference that he attended the meeting on 28 November 1759 must be discounted for his ship sailed for England on 18 October 1759.

It is more than likely, however, that before leaving Quebec Dunckerley attended meetings of the regimental lodges and suggested they should all meet to elect a Grand Master, and in anticipating the outcome of the proposed meeting he was asked to approach Grand Lodge for a provincial warrant. To support this theory is the fact that the request for 'proper sanction' was directed to the Moderns Grand Lodge of England to which Dunckerley held allegiance and not to the Antients Grand Lodge or to the Grand Lodge of Scotland.

It seems to be more than a coincidence that when in London in January 1760 to attend the funeral of his mother he obtained the patent to regulate masonic affairs in the newly acquired Canadian provinces and, indeed, in any part of the globe he might visit where no Provincial Grand Master was in control.

By 1 January 1760 *Vanguard* had finished sea victualling in Portsmouth Harbour and began extra petty warrant (re-storing) the next day. This finished on 2 February and she sailed to Spithead where the convoy was forming and left for North America on 7 March 1760.

Back at Quebec, Dunckerley installed Colonel the Hon Simon Fraser of the 78th (Highland) Regiment as Provincial Grand Master of Canada on 24 June 1760. A few months later Fraser was posted back to England and he was succeeded by Captain Thomas Augustus Span of the 28th Regiment who had been deputy to Lieut Guinnett.

Charitable collections were made and given to the widows and orphans of the servicemen and to Canadians who were in distress and this helped to bring freemasonry into good public repute from the very start.

Dunckerley had become known and respected in Grand Lodge in London and, unknown to him of course, he had secured for himself a place in masonic history as the first ambassador of the Craft and the brother who took freemasonry to sea.

6

SEA GOING LODGES

WHETHER OR NOT Dunckerley was able to attend the quarterly meeting which was held at the Crown & Anchor Tavern in the Strand on 14 January 1760, three days after the funeral of his mother, it is certain he made contact with Grand Lodge; the issue of the 'Provincial' warrant and the authority dated 16 January to hold a lodge on board HMS *Vanguard* being ample proof.

He held the first ever lodge on board a man-o'-war in the *Vanguard* and in the possession of Loyal Lodge No 251 at Barnstaple in Devonshire is a photocopy of a hand-written certificate signed by Dunckerley as Master relating to the initiation of a Brother Edward Gray on board *Vanguard* on 2 October 1760.

It is recorded in the Loyal Lodge minute book that this copy was presented to them on 7 November 1921 by Brother H. Watts, a Past Master of London Lodge No 108 which is directly descended from the Vanguard Lodge, Dunckerley being the first Worshipful Master in 1768, using the Vanguard warrant the date of which is given as the founding date of London Lodge.

The Loyal Lodge Minute says

> The original certificate was discovered by W.Bro. Admiral Halsay at Quebec where Bro. Thomas Dunckerley sailed shortly after performing the above ceremony. A hearty vote of thanks to W.Bro. Watts was passed and it was decided to have the certificate framed and hung.

To make a slight correction to this entry, it is pointed out that *Vanguard* was at Quebec when Gray was made a Mason.

A brother named Edward Gray was admitted a member of St Peter's Lodge, Montreal, which was warranted by the Provincial Grand Lodge of Quebec in 1768 and numbered 223 on the Grand Lodge of England roll. If this was the same man it could account for the original certificate being in Canada, the property of the Public Archives Office in Ontario.

Brother Watts was probably prompted to present the copy of the certificate to the Barnstaple lodge for it has an original oil painting of Dunckerley and the two are displayed adjacent to each other.

I am indebted to the Worshipful Master and to W Bro Malcolm Shaw, secretary, for the following entry dated 14 February 1914, in the minute book of London Lodge.

> A letter dated 10th February 1914 was received from the R. W. Deputy Grand Master the Rt. Hon. Thomas Frederick Halsay (an hon. member of London 108) in which he stated his son Bro. Captain Lionel Halsay, R.N., during a voyage around the world in command of H.M.S. New Zealand visited Ottawa and inspected in a museum or record office a certificate of the initiation, passing and raising of a brother (Edward Gray) in the Lodge on board H.M.S. Vanguard dated 16th. October 1760. The curator having sent Captain Halsay a photographed copy of the original certificate, which was signed by Bro. T. Dunckerley the first W.M., the Wardens and the Secretary, the London Lodge was asked to accept this photographed copy by the R.W. Deputy Grand Master. The copy was subsequently handed to the Lodge by the Deputy Grand Master.

The photograph of the original certificate is now with the lodge records at Freemasons' Hall. The certificate is headed, 'And the Darknefs Comprehendeth it not. In the East a Place full of light where reigneth Silence and Peace'.

The text of the certificate reads

> This Lodge held on board His Majesty's Ship the Vanguard Constituted by Warrant from the Right Worshipfull and Right Hon'ble the Lord Aberdour Grand Master of Masons.

Figure 2
The Certificate signed by Dunckerley relating to the initiation of Brother
Edward Gray on board HMS *Vanguard* on 2 October 1760

We the Master Wardens and Secretary of the said Worshipfull Lodge, Dedicated to St. John Adorn'd with all the Honours and Afsembled by the Misterious Members of the said Lodge.

Do declare, Certify and Protort to all Men Enlightened and Spread over the face of the Earth, That our well beloved Brother Edward Gray, was received and Enter'd Apprentice the Second day of October 5760 and Fellow Craft in this Lodge on the Nineth day of the same Month and year and that after having sustained with Strength, Firmnefs, and Courage the most Painfall Works and Severest Tryals, we gave unto him the most Sublime Degree of Master: and hath Admitted and Initiated as such the above into the Misterious and Most Secret works of Free and Accepted Masons that by his skill and knowledge in Mafonry he may Contribute to the well being and good account thereof he having afsisted us with his Talents and Knowledge.

In Witnefs whereof we have hereunto set our hands and seals this 16 day of October in the year of Masonry 5760.

The use by Dunckerley of the term 'Sublime Degree of Master' is of great interest. It first occurred in a certificate issued by the Grand Lodge of Ireland sometime before 1754 and there is no record of it having been used in England. The description was probably acquired by Dunckerley from a military lodge which he attended in Quebec.

It is possible that Dunckerley held other lodges in HMS *Vanguard* but the possibility of other certificates coming to light is very remote.

The warrant given to Vanguard Lodge was numbered 254 and when he was transferred to HMS *Prince* on 27 March 1761 Dunckerley used this warrant until a separate one was issued for HMS *Prince* on 22 May 1762 with 279 as the number.

Before it arrived, Dunckerley initiated and passed a candidate on 29 March 1762 and raised him the following month. How he overcame the difficulty of having at that time no warrant for the *Prince* can be seen from the wording on the certificate.

Know ye, that having authority from the R.W. John Revis, Esqr., D.G.M. of the Most Ancient and Honourable Society of Free and

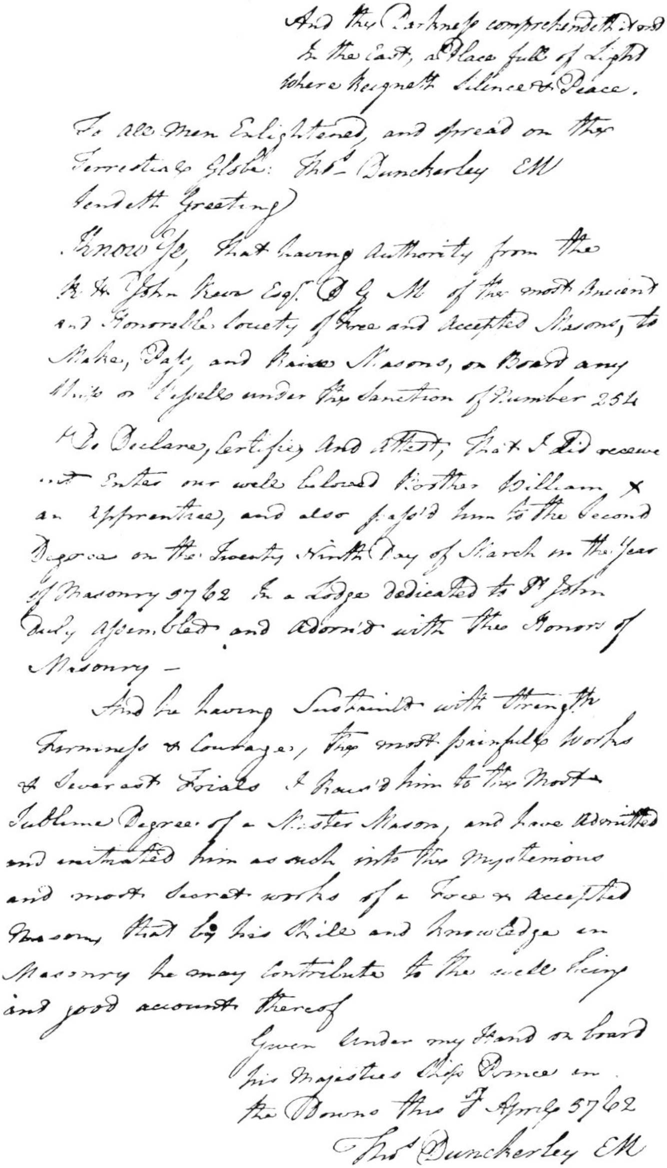

And the Darkness comprehendeth it not
In the East, a Place full of Light
Where reigneth Silence & Peace.

To all Men Enlightened, and spread on the
Terrestrial Globe: Tho.s Dunckerley EM
sendeth Greeting

Know Ye, That having Authority from the
R.t H.n John Kean Esq.r D.G.M. of the most Ancient
and Honorable Society of Free and Accepted Masons, to
Make, Pass and Raise Masons, on Board any
Ships or Vessels under the Sanction of Number 254

I Do Declare, Certifie, and Attest, That I Did receive
into Enter our well beloved Brother William +
an Apprentice, and also pass'd him to the Second
Degree on the Twenty Ninth Day of March in the Year
of Masonry 5762 In a Lodge dedicated to St John
duly Assembled and Adorn'd with the Honors of
Masonry —

And he having Sustained with Strength
Firmness & Courage, the most painfull Works
& Severest Trials I have Rais'd him to the Most
Sublime Degree of a Master Mason, and have Admitted
and entrusted him as such into the Mysterious
and most Secret works of a Free & accepted
Mason, That by his Skill and knowledge in
Masonry he may contribute to the well being
and good accounts thereof

Given Under my Hand on board
His Majesties Ship Prince in
the Downs this 7 April 5762
Tho.s Dunckerley EM

Figure 3
A Certificate issued by Thomas Dunckerley in 1762 for a lodge on board
HMS *Prince*

Accepted Masons, to Make, Pass and Raise Masons, on Board any Ship or Vessell under the Sanction of Number 254 I do Declare, Certifie, and Attest, that I did receive and enter our well beloved Brother William X an Apprentice, and also passd him to the Second Degree on the Twenty Ninth Day of March in the year of Masonry 5762 In a Lodge dedicated to St. John Duly assembled and Adorn'd with the Honors of Masonry.

And he having sustained with Strength, Firmness and Courage, the most painfull Works and Severest Trials, I Rais'd him to the Most Sublime Degree of a Master Mason, and have admitted and initiated him as such into the mysterious and most Secret works of a Free and Accepted Mason, that by his skill and Knowledge in Masonry he may Contribute to the well being and good account thereof.

This tells us the authority Dunckerley had received from Grand Lodge, 'to Make, Pass and Raise Masons on board any ship or vessell'. It was also very personal, 'Having authority . . . I did receive and enter . . .'.

Why was the candidate described as William X? One can only surmise an answer. It could be Dunckerley did not know his surname. Perhaps William himself did not know it as was often the case with illegitimate children, or being unable to write used 'X' as his signature.

At the time of the ceremony HMS *Prince* was in home waters, for the certificate was signed,

> Given Under my Hand on board
> His Majesties Ship Prince in
> the Downs this 7 April 5762
>
> Thos Dunckerley EM

The Downs was an anchorage on the east coast of England inside the Goodwin Sands between the north and south fore-land. It was popular in the days of sail for protection from the easterly and westerly winds was thus provided. It was also a wartime convoy assembly area and a convenient anchorage for ships operating in the North Sea.

The certificates prove Dunckerley's direct association with

two blue water lodges. Altogether there have been three but there is no evidence of Dunckerley being the instigator of the third. It was constituted by the Provincial Grand Lodge of Quebec in 1768 for HMS *Canceaux*, a small ship of only ten guns and a crew of 45 which was being used for surveying the New England coast.

By the time this lodge was created Dunckerley had left the Royal Navy but it cannot be wrong to assume it was created by his example. The Canceaux Lodge was struck off the role in the year 1792.

A lodge met in HMS *Guadaloupe* in which Dunckerley went to the Mediterranean as a 'passenger'. This, perhaps, cannot qualify as a separate lodge, for warrant No 279 which was issued for HMS *Prince* was issued by Dunckerley, probably with the sanction of Grand Lodge or because it had been placed in his custody for safe keeping. On the other hand, the lodge could have met under the authority held by Dunckerley to make masons 'in any ship or vessell'.

The Committee of Charity (now known as the General Purposes Committee) of Grand Lodge met on 22 January 1766 and among the lodges represented was, 'His Majesty's Ship Guadaloupe'. Dunckerley had returned from the Continent and if the names of the masters or lodges representatives had been recorded his would have been among them. The Engraved Lists give a clue. That for 1764 described warrant number 179 as being on board HMS *Guadaloupe* 'on the 4th Wednesday, a Master's Lodge at Plymouth'. The previous list gave it as aboard HMS *Prince*. This however, cannot be taken as evidence that a Guadaloupe Lodge was constituted.

Holding a lodge on board ship must have presented many difficulties, some blatantly obvious. Tyling a lodge in a ship crammed with men must have been difficult and finding space amid the stores, sails, ammunition and guns must have been an even bigger problem. It was as well that there were not the perambulations of present-day ceremonies.

Captain's permission, too, was probably obtained, for a number of members of the crew gathering behind closed doors or a secluded corner could suggest a mutinous motive and for this the punishment was stringent!

It is not known if Captain Swanton of *Vanguard* was a Mason but he had a son (who chose a military career and became a colonel) who was 'made' in the Lodge of Friendship No 3.

There were no difficulties from superior officers in the case of *Guadaloupe* for the captain, the Hon John Ruthven, had been initiated in the Royal Navy Lodge No 282 at Deal on 7 September 1762. He was then aged 22 and before had been given command of *Terpsichore*, a frigate captured from the French. John Ruthven was a son of Lord Ruthven and his maternal grandfather was the Earl of Bute. He was only 24 when he was promoted to the *Guadaloupe*, a sloop of 32 guns and with a length of 109 feet. She had been launched at Plymouth on 5 December 1763.

The Grand Lodge charge for the Vanguard warrant was £2 2s and Grand Lodge accounts also show the receipt of £2 2s to the Fund of Charity from the lodge on 5 June 1761.

What eventually became of the warrants for HMS *Vanguard* and *Prince*? They were used to start two famous shore lodges. The warrant which had been issued for HMS *Prince* was used for the Somerset House Lodge. This new lodge appeared in the Engraved List as No 279 (the *Prince* number) transferred from HMS *Guadaloupe*. In 1774 the lodge absorbed the Old Horn Lodge and is now the Royal Somerset and Inverness Lodge No 4. The *Vanguard* warrant, as already stated, started the London Lodge No 108. The London Lodge and the Somerset House Lodge, regarding themselves as 'sister lodges', had reciprocal visiting without a fee.

The Royal Somerset House and Inverness Lodge meets at Freemasons' Hall, London and the lodge has Time Immemorial status. Lodge 108 meets at Colonial House, Mincing Lane, London.

7

FORMATIVE YEARS

IT WAS FIVE years since Dunckerley had left Plymouth for the North American station in 1758. It was perhaps the five most momentous and masonically formative years in his life.

The Marine Lodge had opened on 2 January 1759 at The Red Lion Tavern in Southside Street, Plymouth, but soon after transferred to a new tavern nearby, the Three Crowns, which was to become one of the most popular masonic venues in the West Country. The hotel is now scheduled as of historic interest.

Soon after his return Dunckerley became the Master of the Marine Lodge which afforded some compensation for the fact that he had missed the opening which he had hoped to perform and for which he had prepared a special ceremony.

The lodge was at that time known as a geometric lodge, as Dunckerley's ritual was based upon that science, and the moral lessons to be learned from it, particularly in the Fellow Craft degree.

In 1780 the name of the Marine Lodge was changed to Fortitude and now thrives as No 105 and still meets in Plymouth but unfortunately its earliest minute book extant dates from only 1848. Then in the 1939–1945 war more valuable documents were lost in the blitz on Plymouth.

Fortunately a considerable amount of reliable information had been collated by a past master, the late W Bro S. J. Bradford PAGDC, who was a student of masonry for more than 60 years and when the Grand Lodge Librarian, Sir Tudor Craig, died in the early part of the Second World War he was asked and consented to help the Assistant Librarian. Some of the knowledge he acquired is incorporated in a booklet *A Short History of the Lodge of Fortitude No 105 1759–1959.*

Brother Bradford was initiated in the Lodge of Fortitude in May 1895 and immediately formed a lasting friendship with the Chaplain, W Bro Samuel Jew who had been initiated in 1848 and had known some who had been members since the previous century, and this proved helpful for as a Royal Marine, Brother Jew made Dunckerley his especial study and much of the knowledge he gained he later passed to Bro Bradford.

The following is an extract from Brother Bradford's booklet.

Dunckerley . . . undertook the task of writing rituals to replace the catechisms . . . he wrote 26 degrees and 12 Masonic Orders, and even to this day parts of his rituals are to be found but little altered in our Craft, Mark and Allied Degrees. His Degrees were:

1. Entered Apprentice
2. Fellow Craft
3. Mark Man, or Foreman of the F.C.
4. Master Mason
5. Mark Master or Mark Mason
6. Master of Arts and Sciences
7. Architects
8. Grand Architects
9. Excellent
10. Super Excellent
11. Red Cross, First Part. Second Part
12. Sublime Degrees of Royal Arch, viz
13. Preparing Point
14. Dedicated Point
15. Decorated Point
16. Advanced Point
17. Circumscribed Point
18. Royal Ark Masons, etc
19. Masonic Knights Templar
20. Mediterranean Pass
21. Knight of Malta
22. Eastern Knights
23. Western Knights
24. Northern Knights
25. Southern Knights
26. Rosy Crusian or *Ne Plus Ultra*, 5 points

His Orders were:
1. Link
2. Wrestle
3. Prussian Blue
4. Red Cross Knight
5. Black Cross
6. White Cross
7. Elysian Knights, or Order of Death
8. Priests order of Seven Pillars
9. Sepulchre
10. Patmos or Order of Phillipi
11. Knight of Saint John of Jerusalem
12. Knight of St Paul

Under the fifth degree (that of Mark Master Mason) were placed the 18th degree (Royal Ark Masons) and the first two Orders (Link and Wrestle). Later the whole of these degrees from Mark Man were placed under the control of the Holy Royal Arch.

Only two copies of the ritual reputed to have been taken from Dunckerley's original MSS are known to be in existence . . . one was made by Bro John Knight of Redruth after he had completed the 26 degrees on 29th April 1777. It is now the property of the widow of Bro. Captain Frank Latham of Penzance, who died in June 1946. The other copy is in the Library of Quatuor Coronati Lodge, and is said to have been copied from Dunckerley's own MSS. by Bro. P. Pender when he completed his 26 degrees on June 17th 1806. Both these brethren received their degrees and orders in our Lodge (Fortitude) as did several other Cornish brethren introduced by Bro. John Knight.

Brother Bradford recalls that in 1905 the then secretary of Quatuor Coronati Lodge, the world's most famous research lodge, went to Cornwall and examined manuscripts in the possession of Bro R. Pearce Couch, but in subsequent reports did not express an opinion whether the manuscripts were correctly attributed to Dunckerley and he catalogued a copy of the secrets of the 26 degrees and 12 orders in the Library of Quatuor Coronati Lodge as 'MS. Ritual . . . Redruth, Cornwall', with no attribution to Dunckerley even suggested.

Indeed, it should be mentioned that considerable doubt has been expressed that it is Dunckerley's manuscript. On the other hand it is only fair to the memory of the late Brother Bradford to say that he was a very intent and sincere mason who devoted a considerable amount of time to research.

8

THE YEARS OF UNCERTAINTY

DUNCKERLEY WAS IN his 36th year when he was told his mother's death-bed statement regarding his parentage. Many years later he wrote a brief autobiography in which he said the details concerning his birth gave him great surprise and much uneasiness.

Not many days after the funeral he was on the stagecoach with his wife making the long, tiring and often dangerous journey over rough roads from London to Plymouth.

To receive without warning news that his father was the King of England must have been a traumatic and even frightening experience. He probably did not know what to do. There was no time to consult anyone and to act on impulse would have been foolish.

The first person in whom he confided was Robert Swanton, captain of HMS *Vanguard*, under whom he had served for almost three years.

To Swanton the news must also have come as a shock. Dunckerley reports that the captain said 'that those who did not know me would look on it to be nothing more than a gossip's story'.

Captain Swanton could have been saying in a tactful and kindly way that he knew Dunckerley to be honourable and genuine and therefore he believed the story, but others might take a different view. Or he could have been saying 'Cheer up, old chap, there is a skeleton in every family cupboard'.

Early March 1760 *Vanguard* was again heading down Channel and Dunckerley's autobiography continues: 'We were then bound a second time to Quebec, and Captain Swanton did promise me that on our return to England he would endeavour to get me introduced to the King, and that he would give me a character.'

Vanguard, however, did not leave for home until 20 October 1760, arriving Spithead on 1 December. By this time the King was dead.

The autobiography continues. 'In January 1761 I waited on Sir E. W. (Walpole) and asked his opinion, if I was like the late King? But, as he was pleased to say that he saw no resemblance I did not, at that time, acquaint him with my reason for asking such a question.'

This is understandable. Because of his mother's association with Lady Walpole, Dunckerley and Sir Edward knew each other as children, but now, as men, there was a great social gap, one a gunner and the other a man of considerable importance whose appointments had included that of Chief secretary to Ireland under the Duke of Devonshire. A gunner in the navy would normally not be completely at ease in the presence of such a person and concerning such a delicate matter. Walpole, too, probably had no desire to be involved in political intrigue which could bring court disfavour.

There was no time to make further approaches. The seven-year war was causing anxiety and Dunckerley, as a serviceman, not only had to obey orders but also had to maintain his rank as a gunner for he had a wife and family to support in Plymouth.

Dunckerley remained in the Navy until the war ended and on 18 June 1764 was 'superannuated by the interest of Lord Digby'. His Naval service was over and acknowledged, but troubles lay ahead.

He was a really desperate man and his story tells us of his financial difficulties.

His royal father was dead; Mrs Pinkney had died some 15 months after his mother and (to quote). 'I knew of no person living who could authenticate the story she had told me; and, as I was unskilled in the ways of court, I saw no probability of gaining access to the royal ear or his Majesty's belief of what I had been told concerning my birth.'

The knowledge that he was the son of a king had not so far helped him. To the contrary it had given him 'A pride that rose superior to my station in the Navy'. In other words he had lived beyond his means and had got badly into debt, to the extent of £300 which was a considerable sum at that period.

Factors contributing to this were an accident sustained by his daughter which led to her having the right leg amputated above the knee and the non-payment by the Admiralty of £130 he had expected as pay as teacher of mathematics in HMS *Vanguard*. The appointment had been made by the Admiral of the Fleet but not confirmed by Lord Anson, the Lord of the Admiralty.

Creditors were pressing, and the thought of incarceration in the debtors' jail was uppermost in his mind, for his story continues.

Fearful of being arrested, I left the Kingdom in August 1764; and, having ordered the principal part of my superannuation pension for the support of my wife and family during my absence, I sailed with Captain Ruthven, in the Guadaloupe for the Mediterranean; and here it was that I had the happiness to be known to Lord William Gordon, who was going to join his regiment at Minorca.

In June 1765, I was put on shore at Marseilles, being seized with the scurvey to a violent degree; but by the blessing of God, and the benefit of that fine climate, I was perfectly restored to health in less than six weeks, when I received a letter from Captain Ruthven, inclosing a recommendation of me to his Excellency Colonel T. (Townsend) at Minorca.

I took an opportunity of sailing for that island, and waited on Colonel Townsend, who received me with great friendship. I remained there six weeks, during which time I was constantly at his Excellency's table; but no employment was offered that was in his power to dispose of.

I had (in the confidence of friendship) acquainted several officers in the army and navy with the account I had received from Mrs. Pinkney, and they were all of the opinion I should endeavour to get it represented to some of the Royal Family.

Some gentlemen of the Lodge at Gibraltar, knowing my distress, sent me £20 to Minorca; and on the same day I received a letter from Mr. Edward M. at Marseilles, with an order to draw on him for £10.

Thus being enabled to undertake a journey through France, I resolved to return to England, and try to get my case laid before the Duke of Cumberland.

I sailed from Minorca on the first of October, and landed two days after at Toulon, whence I went through Marseilles to Nismes, in Languedoc, to wait on Captain Ruthven and my good friend Mr. M. Captain R. gave me a letter to Admiral Keppel (then a Lord of the Admiralty), requesting his assistance for my obtaining £130 due to me for having taught the mathematics on board the Vanguard, and after staying three days at Nismes, I set out for Paris.

When I entered the capital of France, I had only two louis d'ors left, and a small bill which Mr. M. had insisted on my taking.

Soon after I came to Paris I had the honour of an invitation to breakfast with Lord William G. (Gordon) at l'Hotel Deltragnes. His lordship knowing how much I was distressed, begged (with the greatest politeness) that I would give him leave to present me with £200, assuring me that he should receive as much pleasure in bestowing it as it was possible for me to enjoy in the possession.

My surprise at this instant could only be exceeded by my gratitude to this generous young nobleman.

After staying five days at Paris I went by the route of Lisle to Dunkirk, and thence to Calais, where I arrived on the 5th. of November, and was informed (to my great grief and disappointment) that the Duke of Cumberland was dead.

I embarked the next day for Dover; on the 7th. got to London, and had the happiness to discharge £150 of my debt. I removed my family from Plymouth to the apartment in Somerset House, where my mother had resided near 40 years; and at her decease it was continued to me by an order from the late Duke of Devonshire.

The year 1765 was almost at a close.

That is the story of a remarkable adventure. Dunckerley was almost penniless; the means of travel were uncomfortable and tedious and he was in France at a time when the attitude of some of the inhabitants was anything but friendly towards the British.

It is pleasing that some freemasons at Gibraltar came to his assistance. *Guadaloupe* called at Gibraltar on her way to the Mediterranean and Dunckerley was able to make masonic contact and probably attended a lodge meeting. His first visit to the peninsula was 15 years before and when he was not a mason. His 'Lodge at Gibraltar' suggests the then Lodge of Inhabitants No 285 (1762 to about 1800) but of course, it could have been the Mother Lodge of St John, the first lodge in Gibraltar, which was constituted in 1728, both by the Moderns Grand Lodge.

Dunckerley could not have been exaggerating when he said the news of the death of the Duke of Cumberland gave him great grief and disappointment for the Duke was the second son of King George II and they were therefore half-brothers and had both experienced the horrors of battle, the Duke commanding the army at the battle of Fontenoy in 1745 when he was defeated by Marshal Saxe.

Dunckerley reports that the following year, 1766, he was 'honoured with the notice and friendship of several persons of distinction, who endeavoured to convey the knowledge of my misfortune to the Princess Dowager of Wales and Princess Amelia'. Understandably, no support was received from this quarter.

9

A CLOUD IS LIFTED

WITH AN INADEQUATE income to maintain his family and himself Dunckerley was in desperate straits and on 20 November 1766 he wrote a rather pathetic and humiliating letter to Viscount Townshend, having previously been to see him.

They were about the same age and had both served at Quebec where Townshend had assumed command of military operations when General Wolfe was killed. Townshend was now the Lieutenant General of Ordnance (he later became Field Marshal) and was seemingly in a position to offer employment. In the letter Dunckerley wrote.

> ... permit me to acquaint your Lordship that I waited on Mrs. Poyntz (the mother of Lady Spencer) who said she could almost swear I was the late King's son; and assured me she would communicate the affair to Lady Suffolk and do all she could to serve me. Two months are past, and I do not find that she has been able to do anything ...

He went on to say it was a misfortune to have his birth concealed and that it was a 'misery to me now I know it too late'.

He described his financial difficulties and asked what prospects there were of employment 'in any department that is adequate to my poor abilities, and which would not depress me beneath the character of a gentleman. If the salary was small it would be an addition to my present income (£40 per annum) and I might lay something by for the support of my wife or children that should survive me ...'

31

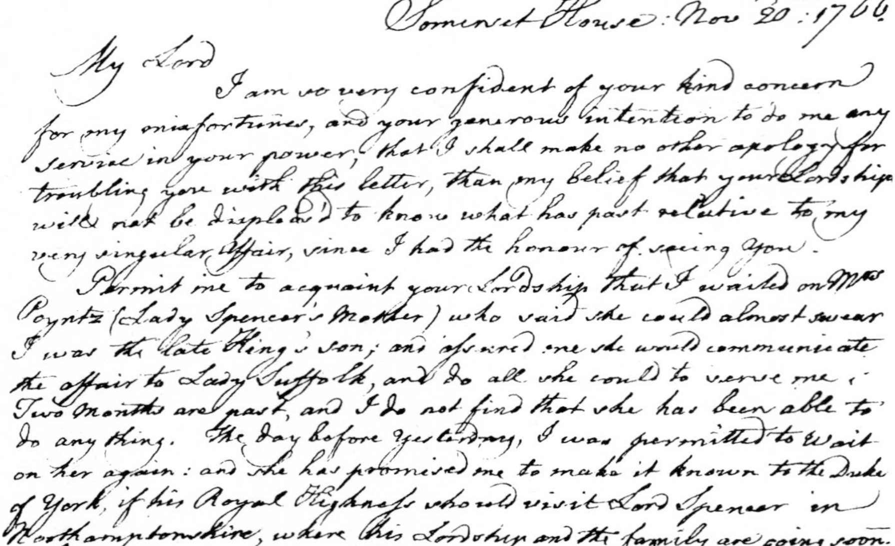

Somerset House : Nov 20th: 1766

My Lord

I am so very confident of your kind concern for my misfortunes, and your generous intention to do me any service in your power, that I shall make no other apology for troubling you with this letter, than my belief that your Lordship will not be displeas'd to know what has past relative to my very singular affair, since I had the honour of seeing you.

Permit me to acquaint your Lordship that I waited on Mrs Poyntz (Lady Spencer's Mother) who said she could almost swear I was the late King's son; and assured me she would communicate the affair to Lady Suffolk, and do all she could to serve me : Two Months are past, and I do not find that she has been able to do any thing. The day before yesterday, I was permitted to wait on her again: and she has promised me to make it known to the Duke of York, if his Royal Highness should visit Lord Spencer in Northamptonshire, where his Lordship and the family are going soon. Lady Barrymore is in Ireland: and I have little dependance on Mrs Poyntz; as her age and infirmities seem to frustrate her good Intentions. It was a misfortune to have my birth conceal'd but it is misery to me, now I know it too late. In spite of all my reasoning, I cannot subdue that pride which proceeds from that consciousness that I am the Son of so great a Man. At present I barely exist, in this Apartment, where my Mother seceded from the World near thirty Years. the smallness of my pension (as a superannuated Gunner) in proportion to the high price of all provisions; and the thoughts of those hardships my Wife and Children must be expos'd to, should death deprive them of their only support; these distresses make me at present a very miserable Being

---

Figure 4
Letter from Dunckerley to Viscount Townshend dated 20 November 1766

I am far from desiring to be troublesome to the Royal Family; or by having a pension, become a dead weight to my Country: even my present distress shall not compel me to wish for that which (to my Conscience) doth not appear right. God hath been pleas'd to bless me with common Sense; which I have for many Years endeavourd to improve, by Reading & Study, not having it in my power to get assistance from Teachers. I should therefore be very happy if I could obtain any Employment, in any Department that is adequate to my poor abilities, and which would not depress me beneath the character of a Gentleman. If the Salary was small, it would be an addition to my present Income (£40 pr Annm) and I might lay something by for the support of my Wife or Children that should survive me. Tho' I have no claim to your Lordship's patronage (according to the present Mode of Interest) yet I address my self to your Humanity, as my Anchor of Hope; most humbly requesting you will recommend an unfortunate Man to the notice of your Brother, or the Marquis of Granby, that I may obtain some little Employ either in the Treasury or Ordnance.

I have taken the liberty of inclosing some of my Certificates, One of which is from that good Man Captain Swanton, who had the honour of being known to you, and with whom you was in company this day seven years past, in the Bay of Biscay. I shall beg permission to wait on You, and have the honour to be, with the greatest Gratitude and Respect

My Lord, Your Lordship's Most Obliged and
Obedient Servant Thos Dunckerley

He enclosed what he referred to as 'some of my certificates' but these were of the non-committal and formal nature issued by senior officers in the armed services, giving the dates in which Dunckerley served in a particular ship and declaring he was a diligent, sober and trustworthy officer.

For a proud man to write such a letter, he must have been under a great deal of stress. In it he mentioned the Marquess of Granby and Lady Suffolk. The former was the Master General of Ordnance and the latter a lady in waiting to the Queen.

As so often happens, the darkest hour was before the dawn and persistence was rewarded. Dunckerley recounted.

> In April 1767, General O (Oughton) (who had known me for several years) acquainted Lord H (Harcourt) with my situation, and that nobleman, with the assistance of Mr. W (Worsley) laid my mother's declaration before the King. His majesty read it, seemed much concerned, and commanded that an inquiry should be made of my Character from Lord C (Chesterfield), and Sir E. W (Walpole) who had known me from infancy. The account they gave me was so satisfactory to the King, that he was graciously pleased to order me a pension of £100 a year from his Privy Purse, May 7, 1767.

Here there is a discrepancy between Dunckerley's own story and the records. Papers in the Royal Archives at Windsor Castle show that Dunckerley received a pension from King George III of £200 a year which, up to 1782, was paid from the 'secret service' or private account in quarterly instalments of £50.

In 1782 the Civil List Act was introduced and curtailed the King's expenditure and this entailed Dunckerley's pension being halved to £100 which was paid by the Prince of Wales (later King George IV), at first in half-yearly instalments of £50 and then in quarterly payments of £25 and continued until his death.

This might have accounted for Dunckerley mistakenly giving the amount of the original pension as £100; his account of events might have been related 20 years or more later. The sailor, however, was home from the sea and comfortably provided for.

Details of payments from the private account were not submitted to parliament and it was, amongst other things, used to provide pensions which, because they were secret, were not subject to taxation and could not be seized by creditors.

In his biography (1972) of King George III John Brooke writes: 'Former servants of the Royal Family . . . literary men such as Dr. Johnson, and poor relations of wealthy families were taken care of in this way.'

Almost overnight Dunckerley's fortunes had taken a dramatic turn. The days of uncertainty were over for he had now an income of £240 a year with little, if any, tax to pay. In addition he had a rent-free 'grace and favour' apartment at Somerset House, being later moved to Hampton Court.

It would seem that R. F. Gould in his *History of Freemasonry* was far off the target when he recorded that Dunckerley received a pension of £100 a year which later increased to £800.

Following the grant of the pension Dunckerley received a letter from Lord Harcourt,

> Sir, I saw General O. last night and am happy to find that we have not been unsuccessful in our attempt to serve you, and hope it will be an earnest to something better. My friend Mr. W. had the happiness to lay your case before a King, possessed of every virtue that can adorn a crown. Don't call on me tomorrow, for I am going to Chatham with the Duke of Gloucester; any other time I shall be happy to see a man possessed of so fair a character, which I value above everything in this life. Your friend and humble servant, H———.

There were also congratulatory letters from the Duke of Beaufort, Lord Townshend and others.

General Oughton, whose endeavours may have been motivated by a sense of fellow feeling for he was the illegitimate son of Sir Adolphus Oughton and a freemason, wrote giving advice.

> Dear Sir,
> I very heartily congratulate you on the happy change you have lately experienced in your fortune. Lord H. and Mr. W. are men whose virtues are of no common stamp, and the bounties of our most amiable and excellent Sovereign cannot flow through channels more worthy of them. It would be a vain attempt, as well as totally

unnecessary to you, to express the sense I have of the King's humanity and goodness. Instances of it frequently come to my knowledge which fill my heart with joy and add fervency to my prayers that it may please God to reward him, even in this life, by impressing on the minds of all his subjects a due sense of their obligations to him for so inestimable a blessing, and affectionate duty to so unparallel a Prince. The attending Lord ——— in Ireland, would not (in my opinion) be an advisable scheme, the expense being great and certain, the advantage small and precarious. Lord Granby may get you a commission for your son, and will, I dare say (recommend as you are), do it readily; they advise you well not to ask a favour of him for yourself. Sir Edward Hawke's proposal is indeed very handsome, and should be gratefully accepted; his motives for making it do honour to you both; but as so sudden a rise will infallibly draw envy upon you, it is of importance that you should be extremely circumspect in your behaviour; a man in adversity is a most respectable character, even a certain degree of pride becomes him, as it makes a greatness of mind superior to ill-fortune, and the world readily gives him credit for virtues which neither hurt their own pride nor clash with their interests; but when the clouds of adversity are dissipated, and the sun of favour shines upon him, he stands in a conspicuous point of view, and the scene is entirely changed envy, malice, and all uncharitableness, find matter to exert their malign influence upon him; the perspective is turned, his faults magnified, his virtues diminished; hence the justness of that Proverb, 'That it is difficult to carry a full cup even,' or as our friend Storace expresses it, 'ut tu Fortunam sic nos te celse feremus'. Humility and complacency are the armour he can put on; but it requires judgment and address to guard against the appearances of meanness or affectation; when those amiable qualities are inherent in the disposition and ripened by judgment, as I am persuaded yours are, the task is much more easy; for the man who acts naturally has always the best chance of pleasing.

I condole with you on the state of Mrs. Dunckerley's health, nor would I wish you to be such a Stoical Philosopher as not to be fully awake to all the tender feelings; but as a Christian Philosopher you will consider that the loss of friends is the condition of life, nor can we hold it by any other tenure. Mrs Oughton joins me in wishing you all possible happiness, and I am,

Dear Sir,
Your most faithful Friend and Brother,
James Adolphus Oughton.

10

AN ENERGETIC PROVINCIAL GRAND MASTER

WITH A GREAT Financial burden lifted from his shoulders Dunckerley was able to turn his undivided attention to freemasonry.

He was not the first Provincial Grand Master, for the rank
dates from 1726 when the Grand Master appointed officers to
superintend lodges, primarily those overseas. It was perhaps an
office which had not been accepted seriously or with the zeal
Dunckerley was to put into the work.

As a Provincial Grand Master Dunckerley was untiring in his
efforts, inducing lodges to keep records and, by example, coax-
ing them to contribute to charity and to the Hall building fund.
His enthusiasm awakened Grand Lodge to an appreciation of
the value of a rank which had been in danger of becoming
dormant in this country.

His first appointment was on 28 February 1767, over two
months before he was awarded his pension from the Court
which dispels any possible suggestion he received the rank
because of his royal connection. The appointment was made by
Lord Blayney who was the Grand Master from 8 May 1764 to
17 April 1767. Not only was the appointment of Dunckerley
one of the last things done by Lord Blayney as Grand Master,
subsequent events have proved it to be perhaps the most important.

Dunckerley had returned from his wanderings on the continent at the end of 1765 and spent the year 1766 resuming his
masonic activities. Having settled his family in apartments at

Somerset House he was much nearer to Grand Lodge than when he lived in Plymouth and probably became a frequent visitor. He would have reported on the use made of the power granted to him to inspect the Craft wherever he went.

The bestowing of this 'inspectorship' in January 1760 indicates he was known to Grand Lodge before then for it would not have been entrusted to a comparative stranger.

He was also still in possession of Warrant No 279 which was issued for HMS *Prince* and also used in HMS *Guadaloupe* and he used this to form the Somerset House Lodge. When returns of masons by name were first called for by Grand Lodge in 1768 those for the Somerset House Lodge included the most influential masons of the time and several of them became founder members of Friendship No 3 early in 1767. Friendship was then meeting at the Sun and Punch Bowl and Dunckerley helped to resuscitate it as an influential lodge with members of social standing meeting at The Thatched House, a St James's Street tavern patronised by the society of the day.

Bro C. D. Rotch in a paper to Quatuor Coronati Lodge in 1943 declared that 'these two lodges organised by Thomas Dunckerley were of outstanding importance in the hundred years following their establishment'.

Lord Blayney, a professional soldier, would have been particularly pleased with the installation by Dunckerley of Col Simon Fraser of the 78th (Highland) Regiment as Provincial Grand Master of Canada and also with the activities of the sea–going lodges and with Dunckerley's masonic activities in the port and Services centre of Plymouth Dock.

Dunckerley now had several associates of good social standing. Further proof of his acceptance into the higher echelons of London freemasonry is that he was introduced to the Turks Head Tavern Royal Arch Chapter on 8 January 1766 by Bro. James Galloway and elected to the Third Principal's chair. Galloway, who was elected First Principal, became secretary of the new Friendship lodge and served from 1767 to 1802. Six months later Blaney was exalted into this Chapter. That same year and the following year some of the most eminent Craft masons were exalted into the Chapter.

In January 1767 Blayney was elected Grand Z of the Holy Royal Arch and Dunckerley was elected Deputy First Grand Principal. The appointment, therefore, of Dunckerley as a Provincial Grand Master the following month is not surprising.

His first Provincial Grand Mastership was, appropriately, of Hampshire. It must have given him pleasure and a sense of pride for it was at Portsmouth that he had been initiated 13 years before.

When he became the Provincial Grand Master the *Book of Constitutions* for that year, compiled by the Rev John Entick, a Grand Steward, defined the duties.

> The Provincial Grand Master . . . is invested with the Power and Honour of a Grand Master in his particular District and is intitled to wear the Cloathing of a Grand Officer, to constitute Lodges within his own Province and in all public Assemblies to walk immediately after the Grand Treasurer. He is also empowered to appoint a Deputy, Wardens, Treasurer, Secretary and Sword Bearer who are entitled to wear the Cloathing of Grand Officers while they officiate as such within that particular District; but at no other time or place.

By this Grand Lodge recognised Provincial Grand Officers, but provincial brethren did not receive Grand Rank until 1887.

Dunckerley's appointments as Superintendent (followed by Mastership) or Provincial Grand Master were.

1767	Hampshire
1772	Isle of Wight
1776	Essex
1777	Dorset
1777	Wiltshire
1784	Gloucestershire
1784	Somerset
1786	City and County of Bristol
1790	Herefordshire

In a letter written from Millbrook near Southampton in 1784 he made it plain to Grand Lodge that in dealings concerning provinces under his control the channel of procedure was through him.

He requested that, 'in future no lodge under my care may be struck off the list before inquiry has been made of me concerning their behaviour and I shall at all times be happy to inform Grand Lodge of the same'.

His letters indicate that it was with efficiency that he dealt with monetary matters, with problems facing lodges, applications to constitute new lodges and more mundane affairs. He made decisions with authority and confidence. In 1784 he erased lodge No 395 'from ye list which I flatter myself the Grand Lodge will confirm'. The members, he reported, had ceased to meet and the landlady (of the Bristol inn where it met) had sold the warrant.

11

SELF PROFESSED SUCCESS

SUCH WAS THE enthusiasm and energy of Dunckerley he was justified in signing letters to Grand Lodge as 'Yr Zealous and affectionate Bro and Serv'.

Writing from his apartments at Hampton Court Palace on 22 November 1785, he reported to Grand Lodge.

> I transmit to you the produce of my labours during the last summer, with an account of £201. 10s which you will do me the favour to lay before the Grand Lodge. The flourishing state of Masonry at Pool in Dorsetshire; and in the Counties of Essex, Gloucester and Somerset, is flattering to me; and I hope and trust that the success I have acquir'd will be equally pleasing to the Society.
>
> Success has follow'd me to the gates of this Palace where, I have (in the space of three months) established a very respectable Lodge.
>
> The Lodges I have constituted at Bath, Bristol, Gloucester and Wells, are daily increasing, and the greatest harmony prevails in those Cities. My endeavours to promote the Dignity and Credit of the Royal Craft, have Cross'd the Atlantic, and I have had the pleasure to obtain Constitutions for two Lodges in Newfoundland.
>
> It was with much regret that I found myself necessitated to erase from my list, the Lodges 339 and 399; which I hope the Grand Lodge will confirm, for the reasons I have given on the other side. The Loans to the Hall Fund, which you will also read to the Grand Officers and Brethren, are expressive of the very great regard those Brethren and the three infant Lodges have for that excellent Institution.
>
> Present my most respectful Regard to the Grand Officers and Brethren. . . .

Lodge No 399, Weymouth, was erased because it was dissolved and the furniture sold, and No 339, Malden, was removed, not having met for several years.

The Bristol Lodge No 472 was forfeited by Thos Tomes, who had partly 'paid for the Warrant, but did not pay the remainder; tho' he made several Masons'.

The following is the balance sheet presented:

	£	s	d
Debt.			
To contributions, &c., ye Charity Fund	26	5	0
Regist'ring Fees, &c., to the Hall Fund	43	9	0
Fees for Constitutions, & Removals	6	16	0
Henry Sperling, Esq., Dennis Hall, Essex	25	0	0
Samuel Tyssen, Esq., Felix Hall, Essex	25	0	0
458 Royal Cumberland Lodge, Bath	25	0	0
462 Royal Gloucester Lodge, Gloucester	25	0	0
474 Lodge of Harmony, Toy, Hampton Court	25	0	0
	201	10	0
Credr			
1785 June 3rd. By paid Bro. Berkley	50	0	0
Oct. 28th By paid Bro. White	50	0	0
Nov. 16th By —Do—	61	17	0
Nov. 18th By —Do—	25	0	0
Nov. 22nd By Balance	14	12	6

Bro. Lewis of Bristol Debtr to Bro White		
Two Constitution Books	£1	4s 0d
Three certificates		19s 6d
	£2	3 6

To attend a meeting at Bath in 1785 he travelled 120 miles over ice and snow. It must have been a nightmare journey in an unheated carriage.

His duties involved a great deal of travel; slow, uncomfortable and expensive. Mostly he used a post-chaise and in his will suggested that it should be sold for the payment of debts and funeral expenses if that should be necessary. He also made use of the stagecoach both for travel and dispatching packages.

In one of his letters to William White, the Grand Secretary, he reveals that in the summer of 1786 he travelled 500 miles visiting lodges under his care in Dorset, Essex, Gloucestershire and Somerset.

But the time and work had brought great rewards for 'Blue and Red Aprons have excited Great Emulation in these Counties and all the Fraternity under my care do me great honour, and are careful not to give offence by irregularity; being sensible it would endanger the stability of their Lodges'.

He went on to say that he was 'not only lov'd but fear'd' and that 'ye preferments on one hand and discipline on the other has produced the money I now send and hope to send'.

The reference to the Blue and Red Aprons is explained by the fact that masters of lodges wore white aprons while Provincial Grand Officers had aprons lined with blue silk with a narrow border of the same material and Provincial Grand Stewards had aprons lined with red silk.

Again writing to White, this time in August 1792, he said.

In the course of 26 years I have worn out 3 setts of collars. I think (entre nous) the Grand Lodge can afford (from the money I shall receive this summer) to present me with a new sett which at all events, I must have next Monday tho' it should be at my own expense – I am therefore to request that you will send addressed to me, to the care of the R.W. Master of the Lodge at the Red Lion, Shaftesbury – 8 collars ready made – by the mail coach next Saturday evening.

The occasion was a Provincial meeting in honour of the 'birthday of our Royal Grand Master'. (The Prince of Wales who later became King George IV.)

12

A Unique Honour

For his services as Provincial Grand Master Dunckerley had conferred on him a unique honour. On 22 November 1786 Grand Lodge granted him the rank of Past Grand Warden, with the right of taking place immediately next to the present Senior Grand Warden.

This, the Grand Lodge minute recorded, was 'in grateful testimony of the high sense the Grand Lodge entertains of his zealous and indefatigable exertions for many years to promote the honour and interest of the Society'.

It was an honour never before or since conferred.

Writing in acknowledgment Dunckerley said he would 'endeavour to return every grateful service in my power'. He said he had served the Society 21 years as a Grand Officer, and 'am now amply rewarded'.

His reference to 21 years' service as a Grand Officer may be a miscalculation. His first mention in Grand Lodge Records was in 1767 when by virtue of his new office of Provincial Grand Master of Hampshire he automatically received Grand Rank.

Twenty-one years before 1786 was the year 1765, and the fact that Dunckerley was wandering on the Continent, having left HMS *Guadaloupe* at Marseilles through illness, supports the theory of a mistake. Four and a half years later he said he had been a Grand Lodge officer for 25 years.

Whether he had been a member of Grand Lodge for 19 or 21 years is of little import for it cannot be denied that he had brought an unparalleled enthusiasm to freemasonry from the day he was initiated in 1754.

13

Dunckerley Threatens to Resign

On 5 may 1791 Dunckerley announced that he intended at the end of the August to resign 'the office of Provincial Grand Master in the several counties over which I have now the honour to preside', and even to leave the Society.

If his threatened action had been put into effect it would have caused a major upset for Dunckerley was at the pinnacle of his career and the peak of his popularity and as he had already said he was loved and feared.

But for the fact that he had promised to hold a Provincial Grand Lodge at Hereford he would have resigned immediately. And it was all due to thoughtlessness and disrespect on the part of a minority of brethren at the festive board following a meeting of Grand Lodge.

Unfortunately the Grand Lodge letter book for 1791 in which summaries of out-going letters were recorded no longer exists, but with Dunckerley's original letters still preserved in the archives it is not difficult to imagine what happened.

Immediately he received Dunckerley's brusque and formal letter the Grand Secretary, William White, consulted other Grand Lodge officers. In reply he wrote what Dunckerley described as 'a very polite letter'. Acknowledging it on 12 May Dunckerley explained.

When I followed my senior to the table every chair was taken, except one and that of right belonged to Bro Lewis. Not any person would make room for me and I was reduced to the disagreeable situation at the end of the table where the dishes were to be handed (over my back) for 200 people, and a door continually opening at my head by which I got a violent cold and have been very ill.

Such treatment, I may say such rudeness, to a man near 70 years of age who hath been 25 years a grand officer and a laborious servant to the Society, and who never was accustomed to scramble for a chair, was too mortifying – too degrading.

It did not become me to trouble the Grand Master with a complaint at the time or to enter into altercation with any person. If you saw me in that uncomfortable place, you had authority by your office to have placed me in my proper seat.

I was necessitated to leave the Hall before the second course was brought on, being unable any longer to bear the crowd of servants at my back. This had determined me to withdraw from a Society where I was treated with such disrespect.

Brother White wasted no time in replying for on 19 May Dunckerley wrote:

I have read your favour of the 14th. and must beg leave to observe that such is the difference between the Grand Lodges of Masons, and the general meetings of other societies (except in London) that our order is distinguished from them by a uniform regularity, peace and harmony.

I have held many Grand Lodges and at some places have been honoured with the company of more than 200 brethren who never experienced the least confusion. Every brother (except the present and past grand officers, with the acting stewards) was seated. When the procession ended the acting stewards halted within a few paces of the upper table. The Grand Master walked to his chair followed in succession by his Deputy, the Senior and Junior Grand Wardens, etc. (in the manner that children play a threading the needle) and the Junior Past Grand Officer was the last person seated.

But how did some of the Past Grand Officers behave on the 4th instant? They left the procession on the third time going round the hall and placed themselves and their friends at the table and in a minute after the present Grand Officers were seated a scramble for chairs ensued.

Dunckerley went on to say Grand Lodge should pass a resolution that to prevent inconvenience at the Grand Officers' table a person should be stationed to prevent any brother from possessing a chair at the table until the Grand Master with the present and past Grand Officers were seated according to seniority.

Grand Lodge adopted this procedure and Dunckerley continued in office and the work he loved so dearly.

I often wonder if it was a disappointment to Dunckerley that he did not become the Provincial Grand Master of Devonshire for he had served as the Master of lodges in Plymouth and Devonport where he was so masonically active. His wife and children had lived there for eight or nine years when he was serving in the Royal Navy.

The first Provincial Grand Master of Devonshire was Sir Charles Warwick Bampfylde who was installed on the 19 December 1775. By this time, of course, the Dunckerley family had left Plymouth and with a threatened invasion of the country by France, who were supporting American Independence, Dunckerley had joined the Army. His next close link with the county was when he became the Grand Superintendent of Royal Arch Masons in Devonshire in 1780.

Such, however, was Dunckerley's reputation and popularity that it was to him that a Brother C. Tenby of Plymouth Dock wrote on 17 January 1793 to make a bitter complaint about 'a shameful abuse of masonry' at the Lodge of Sincerity held at the sign of the Peace and Fame 'where they make any person'.

The letter claimed that two persons were initiated who were sent to Launceston Jail for robbery and declared that the Master was 'a noted sot and drunkard, could neither write or read' and that when he was lodge secretary certificates were signed by other persons 'under his name. Most horrid! What is it but forging and forgery.'

Dunckerley referred the letter to Sir Charles Bampfylde but in informing Grand Lodge expressed the opinion it should be put before the Committee of Charity.

The lodge was the present highly-respected Sincerity No 187 and the Peace and Fame hostelry was in Fore Street, Devonport.

14

GRAND SUPERINTENDENT NONPAREIL

DUNCKERLEY DID AS much for the Royal Arch as he did for the Craft but as Grand Superintendent he covered a larger area, developing the Supreme Degree in the following 18 provinces, serving from the dates shown:

Devonshire	1780–1795
Cornwall	1793–1795
Bristol	1782–1795
Durham	1788–1795
Gloucester	1782–1795
Herefordshire	1793–1795
Kent	1785–1795
Somerset	1782–1795
Surrey	1789–1795
Warwickshire	1793–1795
Dorsetshire	1780–1795
Essex	1776–1795
Hampshire	1778–1782
The Isle of Wight	1778–1795
Nottinghamshire	1793–1795
Suffolk	1787–1795
Sussex	1787–1795
Wiltshire	1780–1790

The earliest minutes of a Royal Arch Lodge or Chapter in this country refer to a Lodge No 220 which met at the Crown in Christmas Street, Bristol, when on 7 August 1758 it recorded

'Brother Gordon proposed to be raised to the Degree of Royal Arch and accepted'. On Sunday, 13 August 1758 at a Lodge 'of immergency Bros. Wm. Gordon and Jno. Thompson were raised to the Degree of Royal Arch Masons'.

Dunckerley was initiated and later exalted to the Royal Arch at Portsmouth in the year 1754, and it has always been assumed that his exaltation was in his other craft lodge, the Three Tuns No 31.

The historian W. J. Hughan puts the date of the Royal Arch as rather earlier than 1744 and the first known typographical reference to the degree appears in a document published 1744 by Dr Fifield Dassigny and entitled *A Serious and Impartial Inquiry into the Cause of the Present Decay of Freemasonry in Ireland*.

The degree made an immediate appeal to him and the certificate presented in 1768 by the Plymouth Dock Lodge (see chapter 4) indicates he had been working the Royal Arch in a Craft Lodge.

The earliest known minutes of a Royal Arch Chapter in London were dated 22 March 1765 and the first anniversary feast was on 8 January 1766. Dunckerley, who was present, was proposed as a member and was elected Third Principal (see chapter 10).

As his royal associations were not yet known the appointment must have been made on his merits and enthusiasm as a Mason. In 1767 the Chapter was formed into a Grand Chapter.

Dunckerley was one of the signatories on 22 July 1766 of the Charter of Compact which constituted the Grand and Royal Chapter of the Royal Arch of Jersusalem which in turn led to the formation of the present Supreme Grand Chapter.

Dunckerley was one of the early First Grand Principals and was untiring in promoting the Royal Arch throughout the country and became First Grand Principal in 1791.

Obviously a man capable of making decisions and acting on his own initiative, Dunckerley, as Grand Superintendent for Wiltshire, wrote in 1780 to inform Grand Chapter he had granted a warrant of constitution for a Chapter of New Sarum and also a dispensation to some companions of the First

Regiment of Dragoons who were then at Salisbury, to hold a Chapter for a year.

Grand Chapter, 'with utmost respect for Companion Dunckerley', considered such grants were exceeding the bounds of his office and they produced a list of instructions, or guide lines, for Superintendents.

The minute recording this ended

A polite letter from Companion Dunckerley explaining his last (letter) in the fullest & most satisfactory manner being read, a Warrant of Constitution was ordered to be made out for the Chapter of Harmony at Salisbury, Comps. Dunckerley, Maton & Burbridge: Principals.

Whenever possible Dunckerley attended Chapters and on several occasions visited the Chapter of Unity No 9 at Bristol, and on 2 June 1786 he presided as Principal and read a part of the Introductions and Sections from his own memorandum.

As in some of the other provinces Dunckerley opened by dispensation the first Royal Arch Chapter in Cornwall. It was the Druids Chapter of Love and Liberality No 79 at Redruth.

The application for the Chapter was made through the good offices of Comp William Harrison, a schoolmaster of Plymouth Dock (Devonport) on 12 July 1791 and on 15 July the dispensation was sent by Dunckerley. The following is a transcription of the document which is still preserved and although still legible the writing is a little too faded for satisfactory reproduction.

By Thomas Dunckerley of Hampton Court Palace, in the County of Middlesex – Grand Superintendent of Royal Arch Masons, &c. To those whom it may concern

Greeting

Know Ye – That at the humble Petition of several Brethren & Companions, residing at, and near the Town of Redruth, in the County of Cornwall; I do hereby Grant unto the said Companions and Brethren full Power and Authority to open, and hold a Chapter of Royal Arch Masons at the Town of Redruth aforesaid, under the Title of the Druids Chapter of Love and Liberality; the stated Days for exaltations, to be on the last Wednesday of every Month. For so doing I grant this Warrant of Dispensation for six Months from the date hereof or until such time as they shall receive their Patent of Constitution from the Grand and Royal Chapter.

Given at Hampton Court Palace this 15th. day of July AL 5795 – AD 1791.

(Signed) Tho^S Dunckerley

| To Compns | John Knight
Peter Pender
Philip Trevena | hereby appointed | (Z)
(H)
(J) | of the Druids
Chapter of Love
& Liberality
at Redruth,
Cornwall. |

It bears Dunckerley's seal in red wax, being 30 mm across and 30 mm deep.

Harrison, who was in the chair of Sincerity Chapter which was then meeting at Devonport, was unable to make the journey into Cornwall to constitute the new Chapter on 16 August 1791 but entrusted the task to Comp R. Tregoning, Principal of the Peace and Fame Chapter at Plymouth Dock who, in a written report to Dunckerley, said 'I constituted the Chapter, Placed the officers and exalted Members of the Druids Lodge of Love and Liberality to the Sublime Degree of Most Excellent Royal Arch Masons'.

On 14 January 1792 Dunckerley wrote to Sir Benjamin Craven to appoint him Provincial Grand Senior Warden of Essex and the Deputy Grand Superintendent of Royal Arch Masons and Eminent Deputy Grand Master of Knights Templar for the county. The following extract is given because of the important information it contains.

The Chapter at Colchester, No. 12, and the Lodge at the Red Lion in the same Borough, I have struck off the List since the death of my much valued Bro. Thos. Boggis, Esq. The Lodge No. 51 have been very irregular and have given me much trouble as our Bro. Abell and other Brethren can inform you, & I have been inform'd that they have exalted Royal Arch Masons illegally (for they never had a Constituted Chapter), and some have asserted that they exalted me. I was Grand Z. of the Grand and Royal Chapter in 1767, and in

1776 when I was Grand Superintendent for Essex I exalted Bros. Boggis, Affleck, Leake, &c. by virtue of my Authority, and some of the Brethren of Lodge 51 – being Royal Arch Masons – assisted. This is the simple Truth & I beg it may be mention'd in the Lodges to crush all false reports concerning me. I was exalted at Portsmouth in the year 1754, & at that time had never seen Colchester.

Bro. Lane at Baintree is a Knight Templar; I believe there are some at Colchester, but do not vouch for any. If you can find a third I will send you a Patent for holding a Conclave.

The letter was reproduced by Henry Sadler in his book (in 1891) with these comments 'This letter is of great historical value and I am under obligations to Bro. G. F. Lancaster of Gosport for the privilege of printing it. Until it was brought to light the time and place of Dunckerley's exaltation were unknown.' It also implies that he was 'Superintendent' of Essex as far back as 1776, and therefore the first holder of that title in Royal Arch, as well as in Craft masonry.

The 'false reports concerning me' referred to by Dunckerley stemmed from some 15 years previous. Only a few documents concerning the early history of the Royal Arch Chapter have been preserved, but among them is a minute dated 12 December 1777, which reads

> It having been represented to the Chapter that Bro. Dunckerley had exalted Brethren at Colchester to the sublime degree, Bro. Smith propos'd that a polite letter be wrote by the Secretary to Bro. Dunckerley, acquainting him of the disapprobation of this Chapter of Brethren being exalted without a regular dispensation for that purpose. Pass'd Nem. Con.
>
> Bro. Leake who having been exalted by Bro. Dunckerley at Colchester applying to be admitted, it was resolved that he be admitted, but that such admittance be not taken as a precedent to others exalted in a like manner.

No doubt Dunckerley replied to this, but it is not difficult to imagine the 'false reports' circulated by those who, perhaps through jealousy, were not kindly disposed to him.

It is amazing, too, how such misinformation persists. As

recently as 1966, when speaking at the bicentenary celebrations of Supreme Grand Chapter, a prominent and able mason, made this comment on Dunckerley: 'He sometimes allowed his zeal to run away with him for in 1777 he was acquainted by "polite letter" of Grand Chapter's disapprobation for exalting brethren in Colchester without a regular dispensation . . .'.

The brother can be forgiven, for he also commented that Dunckerley 'was a most indefatigable worker and the Royal Arch owes much to him'. That is certainly true.

In a letter written by William Hannam as acting Grand Master of the Knights Templar in 1795 we learn that Royal Arch Masons in London wore no aprons when assembled in Chapter and that 'it is proper for the three Sojourners when they are admitted to report their discovery to appear with aprons, but as soon as they are invested with the insignia of their order the apron is laid aside'.

At least two hymns were written by Dunckerley for the Royal Arch. The longer one was sung by the choir at St Peter's Church, Dorchester, when the Provincial Grand Lodge of Dorset gathered to honour the Prince of Wales's birthday in 1781. It was sung to a movement of Dr Arne's in the *Overture to Artaxerxes*.

The hymnn was included in the *Constitutions* published in 1784:

> Almighty Sire our heav'nly King!
> Before whose Sacred Name we bend:
> Accept the Praises which we sing,
> And to our humble Pray'r attend.
> All hail! great Architect divine!
> This Universal Frame is thine.
>
> Thou who didst Persia's King command,
> A Proclamation to extend;
> That Israel's sons might quit his land
> Their holy Temple to attend.
> All hail! great Architect divine!
> This Universal Frame is thine.

The sacred place where three in One
Compris'd they comprehensive Name;
And where the bright Meridian Sun,
Was soon they Glory to proclaim.
　　All hail! great Architect divine!
　　This Universal Frame is thine.

Thy watchfull Eye a length of time,
That wond'rous CIRCLE did attend;

The Glory and the Pow'r be thine,
Which shall from Age to Age descend.
　　All hail! great Architect divine!
　　This Universal Frame is thine.

On they Omnipotence we rest,
Secure of they Protection here;
And hope hereafter to be blest,
When we have left this World of care.
　　All hail! great Architect Divine!
　　This Universal Frame is thine.

Grant us, great God, they powerful Aid,
That Aid will banish ev'ry fear;
For where they Goodness is display'd
Pleasure, Content, and Bliss appear.
　　All hail! great Architect divine!
　　This Universal Frame is thine.

Inspire us with thy Grace divine,
Thy sacred Law our Guide shall be;
To every Good our hearts incline,
From every evil keep us free.
　　All hail! great Architect divine!
　　This Universal Frame is thine.

When the second hymn, taken from the book *Masonic Songs*, which was published in 1885, was composed, it was intended for 'solemn ceremonies' and to be sung to the tune of *God Save the King*.

The words are

> Hail, Universal Lord!
> By heav'n and earth ador'd;
> All hail! Great God!
> Before thy name we bend,
> To us they grace extend,
> And to our prayer attend,
> All hail! Great God!

Just over a month before he died and after 40 years' service Dunckerley wrote to Grand Chapter surrendering his various offices. To do this must have saddened the heart of a great mason and companion who was wearied by sickness and pain.

At all times Supreme Grand Chapter were most respectful in communicating with Dunckerley, yet when he was called to higher service the tributes which one would expect to have been made are not recorded in the minutes.

15

MARK MAN AND ROYAL ARK MARINER

THE NAME OF Dunckerley is associated with the first known reference in a minute book of the Mark degree being worked in England. It is in the introductory minute of the Friendship Royal Arch Chapter No 3 at Portsmouth.

The Chapter, which was warranted on 11 August 1769, is now attached to and takes the number of the Phoenix Lodge No 257 which is the daughter lodge of the Lodge of Antiquity, Dunckerley's mother lodge.

When the Chapter minute was discovered in the early 1890s it was acclaimed by masonic historians, and the famous William James Hughan described it as an 'important find'. It was certainly important and a most fortunate find.

W Bro Alexander Howell, of Portsmouth, was researching for his *History of the Phoenix Lodge and Chapter of Friendship No. 257*, which was published privately in 1894, when he noticed that the first leaf of the Chapter's minute book had been pasted down to strengthen the front fly leaf.

He held the pages against a strong light and discovered there was writing on one of the pages, but it was too faint to read.

Carefully, and with difficulty, he separated the two leaves and discovered 19 lines written in cypher.

He compared the cypher with an old book which was written entirely in cypher, but there was no key to either.

Brother Howell tells the story

Many days were spent in fruitless search for a clue. I then showed the manuscript to a brother who suggested, at a guess, that certain characters at the bottom of the page might be the names of the three principals. The names of the three principals being known to me, I soon found that the number of letters agreed and working with the key thus obtained, succeeded in reading the manuscript.

It is not difficult to imagine the excitement as the cypher was pains-takingly decoded, for the minute is certainly a great contribution to English masonic history and to the biography of Thomas Dunckerley. And to think it was almost lost to posterity.

Where did Dunckerley get this 'mann'r of writing'? Howell put forward the suggestion that it could have been Dunckerley's own invention found on the marks used by the ancient operative masons. This, of course, could be correct. Cypher, in one or another form has been in existence for a considerable time. All the codes are of an elementary nature, based mostly on the arrangement of four lines, as in the case of the children's game of noughts and cross. The 'Portsmouth code' would not have taken Dunckerley long to devise.

The question which may never be answered is where did he receive the Mark which enabled him to make the brethren Mark Masons and Mark Masters? It was probably while serving in the navy when he had the opportunity to visit military lodges in all parts of the world, many of them of the Irish constitution.

The visit to the chapter by Dunckerley certainly left an impression for the indication is that down to at least 1844 no brother received the Royal Arch Degree in the Chapter of Friendship without also receiving the Mark. In the second minute book there is an autographic register of companions with their marks and the minutes were written in cypher, but it is more than likely that Dunckerley gave 'this mann'r of writing' for use only in the Mark Degree ceremonies.

It is a pity there is so little information on Dunckerley's association with the Mark Degree.

The reference to the degree being conferred by Dunckerley at Portsmouth on 1 September 1769 is no proof that he introduced it to this country.

The RW Bro W. Redfern Kelly, who was then the Grand First Principal of Royal Arch Masonry, District Grand Chapter of Antrim (Ireland), expressed his opinion in a contribution to the transactions of Quatuor Coronati Lodge in 1917.

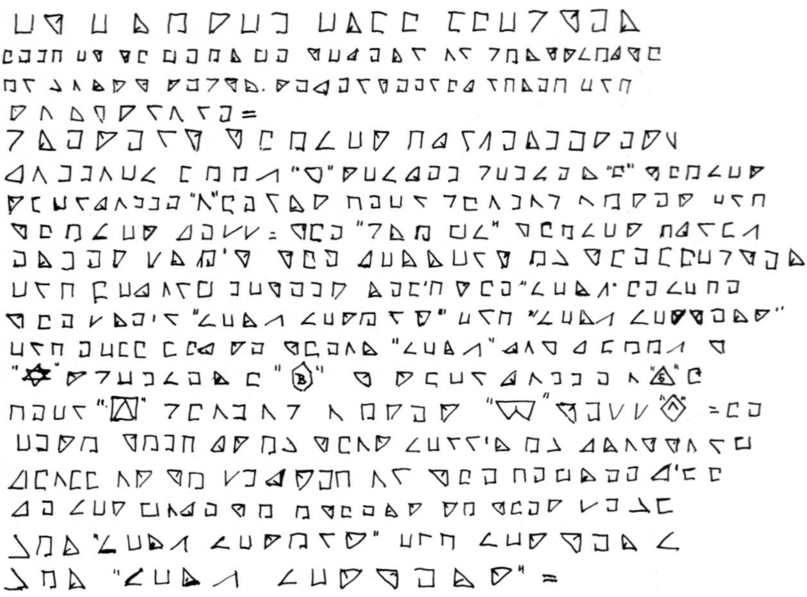

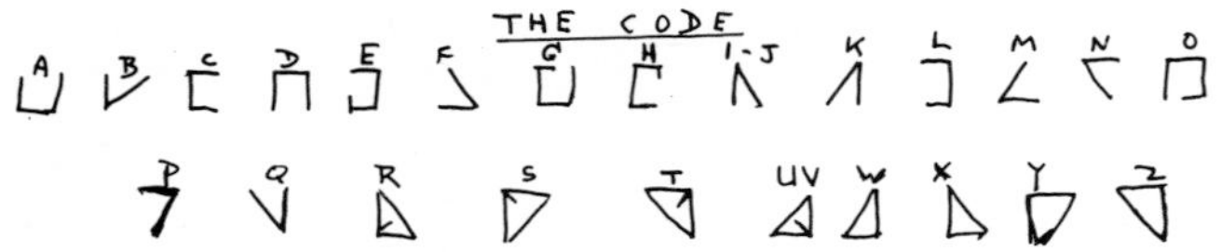

THE CODE

A B C D E F G H I-J K L M N O

P Q R S T UV W X Y Z

Figure 5

The introductory Minute of Friendship Royal Arch Chapter No 3 written in cypher with the code displayed beneath. On the opposite page is the cypher decoded and written in full

AT A ROYAL ARCH CHAPTER
HELD AT THE GEORGE TAVERN IN PORTSMOUTH
ON FIRST SEPTR. SEVENTEEN HUNDRED AND
SIXTY NINE =
PRESENT THOMAS DUNKERLEY ESQ
WILLIAM COOK "Z" SAMUEL PALMER "H" THOMAS
SCANVILLE "J" HENRY DEAN PHILIP JOYES AND
THOMAS WEBB = THE "PRO G.M." THOMAS DUNCK
ERLEY BRO'T THE WARRANT OF THE CHAPTER
AND HAVING LATELY REC'D THE "MARK" HE MADE
THE BRE'N "MARK MASONS" AND "MARK MASTERS"
AND EACH CHUSE THEIR "MARK" VIZ. W. COOK Z

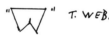

"✡" S. PALMER H "B" T. SCANVILLE J "S" H.

DEAN "◻" PHILIP JOYES "▽" T. WEBB "◇" . HE

ALSO TOLD US OF THIS MANN'R OF WRITING.
WHICH IS TO BE USED IN THE DEGREE WICH
WE MAY GIVE TO OTHERS SO THEY BE FC
FOR "MARK MASONS" AND MASTER M
FOR "MARK MASTERS."

He contended that the degree of Mark Master Mason was invented by Dunckerley in 1767 shortly after the constitution of the First Grand Royal Arch Chapter in England which was mainly due to the zealous efforts of Dunckerley.

He was also strongly of the opinion that the Degree of Excellent Mason might also have been created by Dunckerley in or about 1763.

ROYAL ARK MARINER DEGREE

During the mid 1700s several new degrees and rituals made their appearances, but the names of those who wrote them were not recorded for posterity.

One of these degrees was that of the Royal Ark Mariner and it is suggested that it had a Grand Lodge in 1772. There is so much speculation about the origins of this degree but little evidence to support the theories.

In 1794 Dunckerley was the Grand Commander of the Diluvian Order of the Royal Ark and Mark Mariners. After his death Lord Rancliffe became the head, but he died in 1799 and the degree gradually lapsed until in 1871 it was adopted by Mark Grand Lodge and from then made steady progress.

Now, as a corollary of the Mark Degree it is thriving and has a total membership under the Grand Lodge of Mark Master Masons of England and Wales and its Districts of 23,000.

What pleasure this would have given Dunckerley.

16

NAVAL SERVICE:
FROM BOY TO MASTER GUNNER

IT IS DOUBTFUL if particulars of Dunckerley's early service in the Royal Navy will ever come to light.

He himself provided a list of 'gallant' commanders under whom he served but as some of these were Admirals of the Fleet it was not necessarily in their ships or under their direct command.

He was entered in the muster list for HMS *Namur* as an 'ab' (able seaman) on 14 April 1742. He was then 17 years of age, and this was obviously not his first posting.

As a younger boy he would probably have received quarters and rations with service not accounted for pension.

After the *Namur* his ships and appointments were.

HMS *Edinburgh*	19 February 1744 to 4 March 1746 as Teacher
HMS *Fortune*	20 May 1746 to 1 March 1747 as Gunner
HMS *Crown*	17 June 1747 to 17 April 1753 as Gunner
HMS *Nonsuch*	18 April 1753 to 24 April 1753 as Gunner
HMS *Tyger*	25 April 1753 to 31 March 1754 as Gunner
HMS *Vanguard*	1 April 1754 to 26 July 1754 as Gunner
HMS *Eagle*	27 July 1754 to 25 September 1755 as Gunner
HMS *Vanguard*	26 September 1755 to 26 March 1761 as Teacher and Gunner
HMS *Prince*	27 March 1761 to 31 May 1763 as Teacher and Gunner

The commanders under whom he served, with the Christian names and some relevant details added, were

Admiral Sir John Norris – Admiral of the Fleet 1739. Flagship HMS *Namur* 1739–1740

Admiral Sir Thomas Matthews – C in C as Vice of the Red Mediterranean 1741–1742

Admiral William Martin – Mediterranean 1745. North Sea 1746–1747

Captain Samuel Cornish – Captain HMS *Namur* 1741–1742

Captain John Russell – HMS *Namur* 1742. Died 1743

Captain Geo Berkeley – HMS *Namur* 1744

Captain Coates (or **Cotes**) – HMS *Edinburgh* 1744–1747

Captain Edward Jekyll (or **Jekell**) – HMS *Fortune* 1746–1747

Captain the Hon Edward Legge – HMS *Pluto* 1746–1747

Captain Samuel Marshall – HMS *Tyger* 1753–1754

Captain the Hon J. Byron – HMS *Vanguard* 1753–1757

Captain John Coburn – HMS *Crown*

Captain Robert Swanton – HMS *Vanguard* 1757—1763

Captain Joseph Peyton – HMS *Prince* 1758–1762

Captain Benjamin Marlow – HMS *Prince* 1762–1763

Admiral Sir John Norris was, around the time Thomas ran away, assembling a formidable fleet to assist Portugal who was being threatened by overpowering Spain. It included 25 ships of the line and several frigates and young Dunckerley could have been on board any one of them, anticipating his first experience of war, of man's inhumanity to man. But the very size of the British fleet convinced the King of Spain that he was making a mistake, and he returned to port, with no shots having been fired.

Among those who probably helped in placing young Thomas in the navy was Sir Robert Walpole, for when Thomas ran away it would have been natural for his mother to turn to her former employer and friend, Lady Walpole, for help and guidance. A word from Sir Robert and Admiral Norris, who himself had entered the navy at the age of ten, would have looked kindly on a lad possessed of a spirit of adventure.

Sir Robert's second son, Sir Edward Walpole, certainly helped in later years, for a word in the right quarter speeded Dunckerley's promotion to warrant rank.

Dunckerley, however, certainly started at the bottom as a boy and there was no astronomical rise to the top but what he achieved he did so on his own merits and industry.

The choice of *Honestas et Fortitude* as a motto indicates that young Thomas received a basic grounding in Latin in his few years at school and whatever happened to the boy sailor his education was at least continued for at the age of 19 he was appointed schoolmaster of HMS *Edinburgh*.

This ship, the third *Edinburgh*, was rebuilt from the second of that name. She had 64 guns and was of 1,285 tons and Dunckerley joined her when she was launched in the spring of 1744. Capt Thomas Coates was immediately ordered to sea and to hoist the flag of Vice-Admiral William Martin, who was second in command of the Channel Fleet.

Admiral Martin was a no-nonsense man and demanded a high standard of efficiency from the officers and crews of the ships under his flag. An indication of his character is gained from an incident in 1742 when he was sent to the Bay of Naples to make certain demands of the King of the Two Sicilies. Finding the Neapolitan cabinet inclined to temporise with him he sent his flag captain ashore with the message that Admiral Martin had come 'as an officer to act, not as an ambassador to treat', and that if no satisfactory reply was received within half an hour the British squadron would at once fire and bombard the city.

The reply was received without delay!

As flagship of the detached squadron of the Channel Fleet *Edinburgh* cruised at the mouth of the Channel and all through the year 1745 and into 1746 she was employed cruising between Finistere and the Fastnet, hunting down French privateers and stray French warships. She made several fine captures.

On 20 May 1764 Dunckerley received his first appointment as Gunner – of the sloop *Fortune*. He was then only 21 years of age and the appointment implies that he was a man of some academic achievement and equally important with a personality

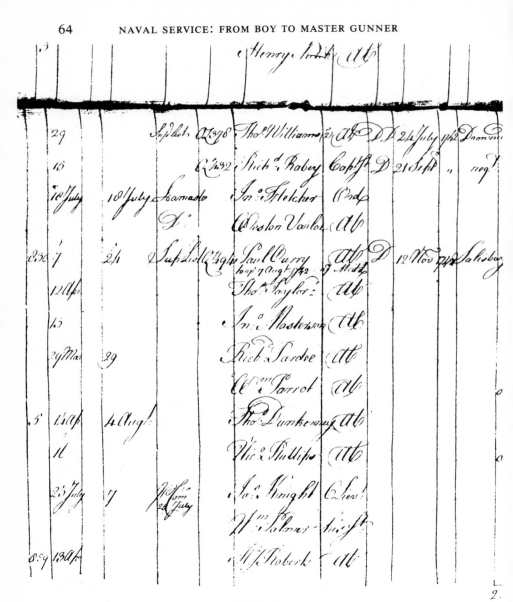

Figure 6
An extract from the muster list of HMS *Namur*, April 1742, showing
Dunckerley as an able seaman

to command. The warrant rank of Gunner was then, as now, one which entailed great responsibilities with the lives of the crew depending on his competence. His commander was Captain Edward Jekyll. Dunckerley was the senior warrant officer and in charge of the ordnance, all fighting equipment and war-like stores and the training of the gun crews.

Dunckerley served in the *Crown* from 17 June 1747 to 17 April 1753 when she patrolled the Mediterranean and he wrote 'in compliance with his Lordship's desire' a series of letters to the Earl of Chesterfield. In these he described visits to Gibraltar, Minorca, Leghorn, Corsica, Sardinia and Barcelona, Malaga, Alicante and Cadiz.

As they are of no immediate masonic value they are not reproduced in this book. Lord Chesterfield was a great statesman and possessed an acknowledged literary merit as his letters to his son Philip Stanhope prove.

What was the bond which established the long lasting and close friendship between these two men of antithetical social status? One answer is that Chesterfield, conversant with court gossip, knew of Dunckerley's parentage and this is supported by the fact that King George III had enquiries made of his Lordship before granting Dunckerley a pension.

For 12 months from April 1753 Dunckerley served in HMS *Tyger* and then for four months in HMS *Vanguard*, a third-rate ship launched six years before. This was followed by 14 months in HMS *Eagle* of 1,130 tons and 60 guns. With a length of 147 feet, a beam of 42 feet and draught of 17 feet *Eagle* carried a crew of 420. Her commanders included at one time George Bridges Rodney, whose name was to find a lasting place in naval history.

From *Eagle* Dunckerley rejoined *Vanguard* in September 1755 and during his service in this ship he came into his own as the Master Gunner. With some 70 guns entrusted to his charge and a large number of men under his direct command, a great onus rested on Dunckerley's shoulders.

Captain Robert Swanton was an officer who searched out the enemy. *Vanguard* was in several engagements and it was a time of great naval victories for Britain.

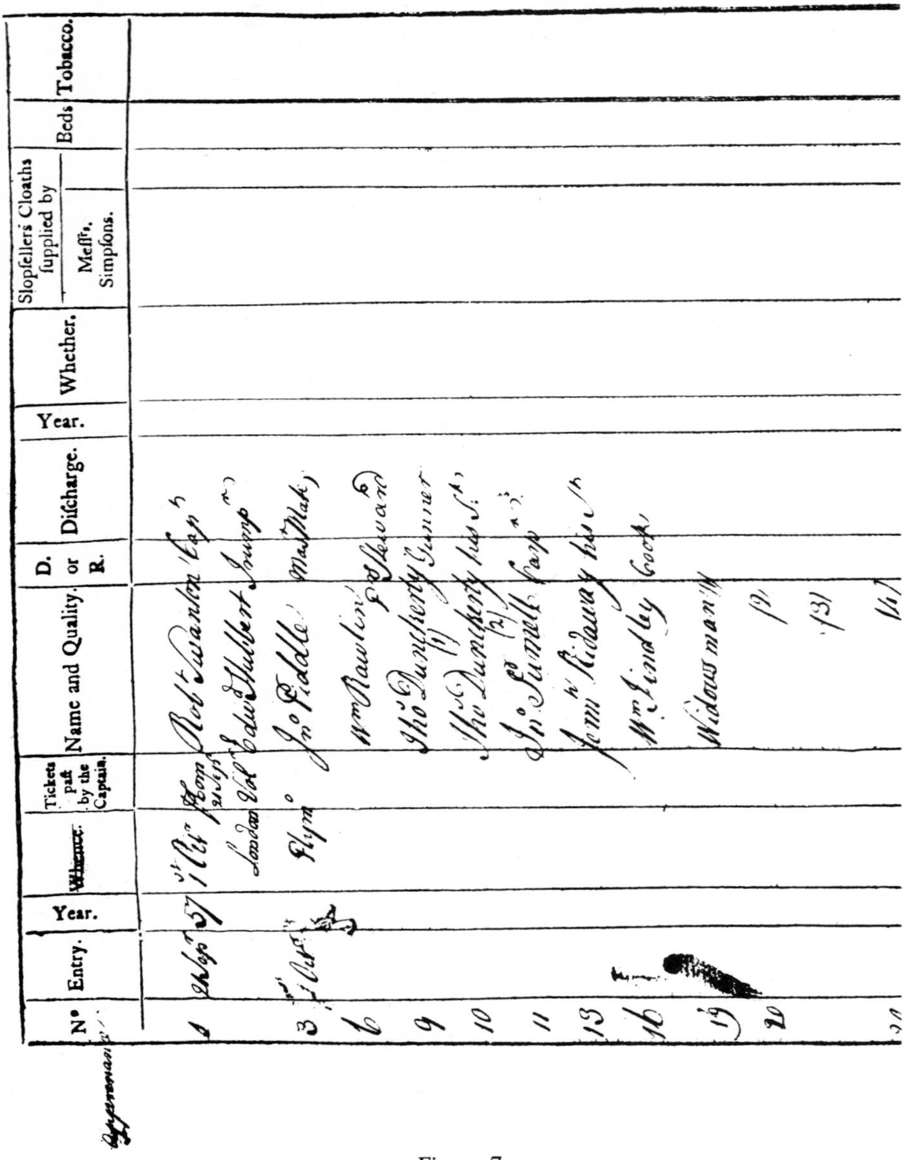

Figure 7
An extract from the muster list of HMS *Vanguard*, October 1757, showing
Dunckerley as a gunner (No 9) and his son (No 10)

When on patrol on 23 November 1757 *Vanguard's* look-out sighted the French Squadron, which was commanded by the famous De La Motte. Swanton immediately gave the order to engage the foe. Dunckerley barked his commands and there was an exchange of fire but the frenchmen, believing that discretion was better than valour, went scurrying into the safety of Brest.

One has a feeling that *Vanguard* was a particularly happy and efficient ship. In her log there were only a few entries of punishments, usually for drunkenness or bad work, but gunnery practise and small arms drill were frequent, and as they polished their guns the men sang sea shanties.

The illustration (*Fig* 6) is an extract from the Muster List of HMS *Namur* of April 1742. It shows Dunckerley as an able seaman. Also reproduced (*fig* 7) is the Muster List of HMS *Vanguard* at Plymouth in October 1757. Numbers 9 and 10 are Thomas Dunckerley, Gunner (1) and Thomas Dunckerley, his son (2).

If Dunckerley was married at the age of 20 in 1744 his son could have been no more than 12 at the time he saw active service, perhaps as a 'powder monkey', and played a part in a memorable victory.

Thomas, the son, left HMS *Vanguard* on 6 March 1760 the day before she left England to return to Quebec. The reason given in the ship's log was 'Preferm (577)'.

17

GUNS FIRED IN ANGER

FOR *Vanguard* and Master Gunner Dunckerley the years of glory really began in February 1758 when she sailed from her home port of Plymouth for Spithead, arriving on 10 February.

A month later she left for the North American Station escorting a convoy of 17 ships crowded with troops and packed with equipment. Something great was imminent and there was an air of excitement and anticipation as they sailed into the unknown. On 9 June *Vanguard* was at New York where the harbour presented a scene of unprecedented activity and for five days she intercepted all vessels entering and leaving.

On 14 June 1758 *Vanguard* left for Halifax and from 4 July she was searching out the enemy at the mouth of the mighty St Lawrence River.

With a favourable wind on 22 July 1758 she sailed in a flotilla up river to Quebec Harbour where, under cover of darkness, French ships were attacked.

The sky became a great red glow as the French ships were set on fire and the water was teeming with sailors as they jumped from their blazing infernos.

For some months *Vanguard* was engaged on patrol and on interception work. She was at the siege of strongly fortified Louisburg, Nova Scotia, when Admiral Edward Boscawen, who was in charge of the fleet, and the legendary General Jeffrey Amherst helped to restore British prestige.

While at Louisburg Admiral Boscawen appointed Dunckerley 'teacher of the mathematics on board the Vanguard' in addition to his rank as Gunner. This unusual procedure of appointing one person to two ranks was quite possibly one way

Figure 8
An artist's impression of HMS *Vanguard* under sail

of rewarding him for distinguished services for it carried extra pay. This should have been £130 for the three years he held the appointment. Dunckerley sadly records '. . . though I discharged both duties for three years to the satisfaction of my captain . . . the pay could not be obtained because Lord Anson had not confirmed the warrant . . .'

In the stress of the conditions prevailing at the time the notification of the appointment probably did not reach Lord Anson who was the First Lord of the Admiralty, or regulations prohibited dual appointments.

One of the greatest honours for HMS *Vanguard* was to give support to General James Wolfe and his army of 8,000 men in the assault on Quebec. On a moonless night this small but gallant force scaled the Heights of Abraham which overlooked the town and in the ensuing battle many brave men fell, among them Wolfe, in his hour of victory. His French antagonist, General Marquis de Louis Montcalm, was also mortally wounded. Two courageous men of opposing sides died on 13 September 1759.

Dunckerley spent his 35th birthday in the North Atlantic for on 18 October 1759 *Vanguard* set sail for England with two other ships under the flag of Vice-Admiral Charles Saunders.

Dunckerley had no idea that in just over two months his mother would die and his whole life would alter.

When *Vanguard* was nearing the British shores there came the not unfamiliar cry from the Crow's Nest 'Enemy in sight'. The French Fleet was also at sea. Captain Swanton crowded sail and was about to go in search, for there was imminent danger of a French invasion of the British Isles, when news was received of the battle of Quiberon Bay when the French had been defeated in a terrific storm.

On 14 November *Vanguard* was off the Lizard; the next day she was sighted from the Isles of Scilly. In dense Channel fog *Vanguard* arrived at Spithead on 30 November 1759 but in a running sea she went aground.

There was no pandemonium for Swanton was not the type to panic, but there was certainly intense activity and with her own boats and the assistance of two other vessels, she was refloated.

after two and a half anxious hours, with no damage.

Refitted and re-equipped at Portsmouth *Vanguard* was ready on 1 March 1760 to escort a convoy to the North American Station. She resumed patrol of the St Lawrence estuary from the base at Halifax, an important but comparatively placid task compared with what was to follow.

The French governor of Canada had devised a plan for the recapture of Quebec by taking advantage of the fact that ice would close the St Lawrence and prevent the access of British ships from the sea, although the higher reaches of the river would be navigable. Accordingly the French, with a large army and flotilla descended the river and came within sight of Quebec on 28 April.

A much smaller British force attacked but heavy losses forced them to retire and the French commenced siege operations. On 15 May *Vanguard* and two frigates came up river and the next day worked up towards the French flotilla and drove them back. A French ship of 36 guns and another of 32 guns were grounded and another burnt.

While her two smaller and lighter draught consorts were engaged in this work *Vanguard* got into position to enfilade the French lines with a vigorous cannonade fired at Dunckerley's commands. The enemy retired, leaving behind more than 50 guns and mortars.

On 1 August 1760, 600 troops landed by boats from *Vanguard* on to the Quebec North shore but were repulsed by heavy gunfire and 27 were killed and 400 wounded – a formidable casualty list. *Vanguard* conveyed the wounded back to Halifax to 'the tent' (the hospital) and took on crew replacements from men discharged from the casualty station and she then resumed patrol.

On 18 October 1760 she joined the fleet at Bird Island (Cape Breton) and left for home on 20 October. For the second successive year Dunckerley spent his birthday in the unfriendly North Atlantic. It was 1 December 1760 when they arrived at Spithead.

The part played by *Vanguard* in this historic action was praised by General Murray who was in command of the operations at Quebec. Of Swanton and two other captains, he wrote: 'I have no words to express their alacrity and bravery . . . The honour they have acquired on this occasion should render their names immortal.' Captain Swanton was later promoted Admiral of the Blue.

Dunckerley's last ship as a serving officer was HMS *Prince*, to which he was appointed by Admiral the Lord Anson and in which he served from 27 March 1761 to to 31 May 1763.

HMS *Prince* was a 90 gun ship of 1,677 tons. She was built at Chatham and with a length of 168 feet was designed to carry a crew of 750. There could have been little room in which to hold masonic meetings!

She was broken up at Plymouth in 1775 after 25 years' service. In HMS *Prince* Dunckerley served first under Captain Joseph Peyton and then Captain Benjamin Marlow.

Thomas Dunckerley was never given command of a ship. If he had, the work of those who research him would probably have been easier. It was perhaps a disappointment to him, but as Brother White, who wrote a 'Sketch' of Dunckerley, explained: '. . . having no parliamentary interest, nor any friend in power, that he knew of, to assist him his own modest merit was insufficient to procure him a command.'

In a large ship in the mid-1700s the Commissioned officers were the Master, Chaplain, Surgeon and Purser and the Warrant officers the Gunner, Boatswain and Carpenter. In small ships often the only Commissioned officer was the Captain.

The voyage Dunckerley made to the Mediterranean in HMS *Guadaloupe* started two months after the completion of his naval service in June 1764, and he probably sailed with Captain, the Hon John Ruthven, as a passenger although he might ostensibly been included on the ship's papers as a crew member to overcome regulations and for the purposes of rations.

Guadaloupe was a sixth-rate ship launched at Plymouth in the previous December. She was 109 feet long. On 10 October 1781 she was sunk to avoid the ignominy of capture by the French.

Some ships have been referred to as of a certain 'rate'. Warships were classified into 'rates' by Admiral Lord Anson when he was was the First Lord of the Admiralty (1751 to 1756). It was based on size and the number of guns carried.

A first rate ship was one of the largest of her time, and carried from 100 guns upwards. The other five ratings were – second, from 84 guns; third, from 70 guns; fourth, from 50 guns; fifth, from 32 guns; sixth, any number of guns up to 32 if commanded by a post captain.

Ships of the first three rates were considered powerful enough to be in the line of battle in action between main fleets. Only a few fourth-rate ships were built, not being sufficiently powerful to be in the line of battle. Fifth and sixth rates were known as frigates.

Fleets were divided into squadrons which in turn were sub-divided into three each denoted by a Red, White or Blue Flag, and with a full Admiral in charge and Vice-Admiral and Rear-Admiral as second and third in command. Squadrons ranked in the order Red, White and Blue and Admirals took precedence according to the colour of their squadron. The 'Admiral of the Red' would be the senior and therefore the Admiral of the Fleet.

It will be seen from the ships' Muster 'Widows men' were included. For these men who never existed pay was set aside to give as compensation to widows of crew members who were killed.

18

RELUCTANT BARRISTER
BECOMES ARMY OFFICER

RETIRED FROM THE Royal Navy, returned from his wanderings on the Continent and financial difficulties resolved, Dunckerley turned his attentions to the choice of a career.

He moved his family from Plymouth to the apartment his mother had occupied at Somerset House. The inference is that it was not large or imposing; he referred to it in a letter as 'where my mother seceded from the world near 30 years'. It had the great advantage of being rent-free and near London and the centre of activities.

A brief account of Dunckerley's life which was published in the *Freemasons' Magazine* in 1793 while he was still living states that

> possessing a strong active mind, with an easy fluent delivery, he was advised in the year 1770, to become a student in the law and during five years close application he acquired such a fund of legal knowledge, that in the Michaelmas Term 1774 he was called to the Bar.

The essence of this is confirmed by the Librarian and Keeper of Manuscripts of The Honourable Society of the Inner Temple. In fact 'Thomas Dunckerley of parish of St Mary-le-strand, Middx. Esq.' was admitted to the Inn on 1 January 1770. He was 'called to the Bar to be utter barrister' as recorded in the Minutes of Parliament (the Inn's governing body) dated Hilary Term 10 February 1774–75. He is also recorded as having his name 'sent for choice of Reader to Lyons Inn, 14 June 1779'.

His name is not included, however, in any of the early Law List volumes, thus confirming that having acquired professional status, he did not pursue a career at the Bar.

Britain was still under threat of invasion by the French who were supporting American Independence and to Dunckerley, a man of action, this apparently seemed to offer a more exciting outlet for pent-up aspirations than the dusty archives of a law chamber.

Although now 50 years of age, he applied for and obtained a commission in the South Hampshire Militia and it is recorded in the *Freemasons' Magazine* article that 'he greatly distinguished himself during three years' service'.

Now, over 200 years later, it is difficult to find evidence to elaborate this. It is seen from the 1779 Militia List that he became a lieutenant in the South Hampshire Regiment on 23 April 1778, but his name does not appear in the 1781 List which is the next one available. Unfortunately no list for 1780 is held by the National Army Museum or the Ministry of Defence Library. It is possible one was not published.

A search reveals that his name is not in the lists of officers of either the North Hampshire or South Hampshire Militia held by the Royal Hampshire Regiment. Neither is he mentioned in Colonel Lloyd-Verney's exhaustive history, *The Records of the Infantry Militia Battalions of the County of Southampton – From 1757 to 1894* which was published at the end of the last century.

In these circumstances it would be rather fanciful to reiterate that 'he greatly distinguished himself' in the Army, although it would be safe to claim that whatever he was called upon to do he did well.

He was proud of his army commission, and on the dispensation he granted to the Medina Lodge in the Isle of Wight in October 1779 he is described as a Lieutenant.

19

His First Province: Hampshire And The Isle Of Wight

When Dunckerley became Provincial Grand Master of Hampshire in 1767 there were the following lodges:

Lodge	Warranted	Erased
Three Tuns, Portsmouth No 35	1724	1838
Portsmouth Common No 242	1759	1768
Isle of Wight No 57	1761	Now Medina No 35
Portsmouth Common No 278	1762	1767
Portsmouth No 291	1762	1773
Havant No 298	1763	1768
Stubbington No 302	1763	1773
Ringwood No 318	1764	Now Unity No 132
Hilsea No 323	1764	1767

There were also two lodges under the banner of the Antients.

Soon after his appointment he constituted a lodge at the New Inn, Christchurch. It was probably the first lodge constituted by him as Provincial Grand Master. It would have given him pleasure to have known that over 200 years later it would still be flourishing for it is now the Lodge of Hengist No 195 at Bournemouth. There are now 222 lodges under the banner of the Provincial Grand Lodge of Hampshire and the Isle of Wight. The province has come a long way on the foundations laid by Thomas Dunckerley.

There was also a less pleasing task. On 27 January 1768,

barely a year after his appointment, Dunckerley had the Havant Lodge struck off for disobeying his orders.

This implementation of his authority indicated his intention to discipline and bring lodges into line. It was repeated in 1771 when he made a report concerning the Lodge of Unity now No 132.

The report was addressed to the Grand Lodge of Free and Accepted Masons of England in Quarterly Communication Assembled, and it said

Right Worshipful and Brethren,

Ever since I had the honour of being appointed Provincial Grand' Master for Hampshire, nothing has been wanting in my power to Excite the Lodges in that County to contribute as much as they conveniently could spare to the Grand Charity; and I have, as I thought it my Duty, constantly Exhorted them to comply with the Laws and Regulations of the Grand Lodge; and to transmit to me, previous to each quarterly Communication a list of their Members, particularly of such as had been lately made Masons.

I am sorry to acquaint you that the Lodge held at the Nag's Head, Lymington, in Hampshire has paid no regard to any of my letters for two years past. I found myself under the disagreeable necessity of acquainting them (last month) that if they did not transmit to me a list of their members, I would certainly have the Lodge struck off the list. They made no answer to my letter: but sent a Guinea to Bro. Heseltine for the Grand Charity, and acquainted him that they had received an impertinent letter from me.

The Deputy Grand Master advised me to propose the erasement of their Lodge at the time, but I have forbore the application near eight months longer. But as the aforesaid Lodge still remains in contempt of me, I am to request of the Grand Lodge to support my authority, by giving direction for the aforesaid Lodge to be struck off the List of Lodges for not complying with the directions and instructions of their Provincial Grand Master, and that all Lodges may have notice of the same, by a copy of the order being printed with the' account of the several contributions to the Grand Charity this evening.

I am prevented by a severe cold the pleasure of waiting on the Grand Lodge, to whom I beg leave to subscribe myself.

Your most faithful and affect. Brother,

Thos. Dunckerley, P.G.M. for H.

The letter was written by Dunckerley from Somerset House and dated 29 November and was read in Grand Lodge in the afternoon.

It was resolved by Grand Lodge 'That the Lodge at the Nag's Head, Lymington be wrote to by the G.S. and acquainted with Bro Dunckerley's complaint, or to settle the matter with Bro Dunckerley by or before the next Q.C.'

A tactful but stern letter must have been written to the lodge by the Grand Secretary for at the next Quarterly Communication of Grand Lodge Dunckerley paid a guinea on behalf of the lodge.

One contemplates what would have happened had a cold not prevented Dunckerley from attending Grand Lodge and making a persuasive speech. The lodge would not, perhaps, have been meeting at the present time at Ringwood, and the Province of Hampshire and United Grand Lodge would have been a good lodge short.

Dunckerley, however, made his point and it was for the good of all.

Life as Provincial Grand Master of Hampshire was not all a bed of roses. Supporters of the established Grand Lodge who were termed the Moderns received anything but masonic friendship from certain of the brethren who ranked under the banner of the Antient or Athols and challenged their supremacy.

In 1786 a Bro Samuel Palmer – who had supported the Antients in their early years – requested Dunckerley to secure a warrant to form the Phoenix Lodge in Portsmouth. This brought the wrath of the Antients on Palmer and in a letter to him a Jno. Gawler wrote: '. . . What mann'r of brother you are is prov'd by your desserting us, and getting that wiseacre Dunkerly to help you get a modern Instn. . . .'

This indicates some of the difficulties which Dunckerley had to overcome.

Taking the view that it was better to have Palmer back under the constitution of Grand Lodge than to have him line up with the seceders, Dunckerley had the warrant issued on 20 May 1786, and Palmer was the first Master.

On 21 August 1788 Phoenix was the host lodge for a Provincial visit to Portsmouth.

Church bells were rung and the Standard flown from the church tower. After dinner at the George Tavern in the High Street, where Phoenix Lodge no 257 held their meetings, several toasts were honoured,

The meeting, says a newspaper report, was 'numerous and very respectable. The day was passed with the regular and harmonious hilarity peculiar to the Royal Craft. It was the Feast of Reason and the Flow of the Soul'.

There were 17 members of the Phoenix Lodge present, 18 visitors, several of whom were from the Three Tuns Lodge, some from the Royal Navy Lodge at the Sea Horse Tavern and one from Prince George Lodge No 86, Plymouth.

The day was the 23rd birthday of the Prince who was the third son of George III, later to become William IV, on 9 March two years before he was initiated in the Prince George Lodge at Plymouth.

There were several other happy and memorable occasions in Hampshire. At the request of the Corporation he laid the corner-stone of All Saints Church at Southampton on 3 August 1792. It was done with full masonic pomp and ceremony, the brethren coming from all parts of the county to take part.

Nearly 60 brethren of the Southton Lodge (named the Royal Gloucester Lodge in 1820) applied to take part but as they had been warranted in 1772 by the Antients Dunckerley refused their request unless, he said, they pledged allegiance to the Moderns and to Grand Lodge.

Within a matter of hours the brethren petitioned for a constitution and were immediately granted a dispensation and took part in the procession.

The lodge then worked under both constitutions, never able to decide which side to accept wholely and solely. They also kept two minute books! Now the holder of a bicentenary warrant and the No 130 the Lodge still meets at Southampton, unreservedly loyal to the United Grand Lodge of England. It was at any rate a partial victory for Dunckerley!

THE THREE TUNS LODGE

Dunckerley's mother lodge, founded in London in 1724, moved to Hampshire five years later and was the first lodge to meet there and following the custom of those days it took the name of the tavern where it assembled – The Three Tuns.

The Lodge at the Three Tuns was registered by the Modern Grand Lodge as No 35 and in 1788 was given the title of Lodge of Antiquity.

Although he did not continue his membership, Dunckerley retained an affection for his mother lodge and it caused him great disappointment when it was erased on 23 April 1773. According to Sadler's *Masonic Facts and Fiction* this was because members were 'being very mutinous and most irregular in making returns' and up to then had been kept on the Grand Lodge list by the personal influence and private contributions of Dunckerley himself. On his insistence the lodge was reinstated the following year and continued to work until September 1838, long after the death of its most famous initiate.

The circumstances of its final closure are recorded in the Grand Lodge letter book (into which letters were copied).

These extracts are from a letter dated 15 July 1840 sent by the Grand Secretary (W Bro W. H. White) to Rear-Admiral Sir Lucius Curtis, then Deputy and later Provincial Grand Master of Hampshire.

> Prior to the erasure of the Lodge I endeavoured to impress upon some of the brethren of Portsmouth the desirableness of endeavouring to keep the Lodge alive, it being the oldest in the county . . . The last two letters addressed to the Lodge were summonses sent by order of the Grand Lodge calling upon the Master &c. to make their returns within a given period . . . both these letters were refused to be taken in, and were consequently returned here through the Post Office. The Grand Lodge then permitted the case to stand over til September 1838, when the order for erasure was passed. The last return from the Lodge was up to March 1831.

It is unfortunate that the Lodge of Antiquity, which could have been a lasting memorial to a great freemason, was allowed to lapse. Still surviving, however, is its 'daughter' lodge, Phoenix No 257, which continues to meet at Portsmouth and celebrates its bicentenary in 1986.

The numbers alloted to the Lodge of Antiquity were

$$
\begin{array}{ll}
35 & \text{in } 1724 \\
31 & \text{in } 1740 \\
21 & \text{in } 1755 \\
20 & \text{in } 1770 \\
18 & \text{in } 1780 \\
17 & \text{in } 1792 \\
28 & \text{in } 1814 \\
26 & \text{in } 1832
\end{array}
$$

THE ISLE OF WIGHT

Although it had only one lodge, the Medina, which dated from the early 1730s, the Isle of Wight was made a separate province in 1772 and Dunckerley was given responsibility.

He had already had trouble with this lodge and had himself made payment on behalf of the lodge to Grand Lodge. The lodge remained negligent and taking a stern hand, Dunckerley had it erased in 1773 for non-payment of dues.

It was reinstated in 1779 and Dunckerley presided over the meeting that year, but the fact that from 1780 to 1787 it retained the same Master indicates a lack of enthusiasm and a small membership.

In the hope of reviving freemasonry on the Island Dunckerley appointed Edward Rushworth as his Deputy Provincial Grand Master but this brother did little to help and was replaced by the long-serving Master, W Bro W. Holloway, and for a time the fortunes of the lodge improved.

Despite subsequent setbacks it is still functioning at Cowes today as Lodge No 35. The oldest of the present 16 lodges on the island, it owes a great deal to the patience and persistence of Thomas Dunckerley.

Six weeks after taking office Dunckerley made his first recorded attendance at a meeting of Grand Lodge, his name appearing in the minutes as 'Thomas Dunckerley PGM for the County of Hampshire'.

In 1776 Dunckerley installed his Deputy, Lord Charles Montagu to succeed him, but eight years later his place was taken by Captain W. H. Pascal. On the death of Pascal in 1786 Dunckerley again took over as Provincial Grand Master.

Dunckerley's appointment as Provincial Grand Master for the second time was the result of several letters from Hampshire lodges to London. The Lodge of Concord, Southampton, wrote: 'It is requested of the R.W.M. & Brethren of the Lodge of Concord held in this Town, that Thos. Dunckerley, Esq., be appointed Provincial Grand Master for this County in the Room of Capt. Pascal deceased; which request I was desired to transmit to you some time back, but being busy it escaped my memory . . .' The secretary requested that the 'business be forwarded as fast as possible'.

20

SERVED ESSEX FOR TWENTY YEARS

THE LONGEST REIGN as Provincial Grand Master by Dunckerley was over Essex to which he was appointed in 1776 and served for almost 20 years. Before his appointment Essex had been supervised by the Grand Secretary.

There were four lodges – Angel No 64, Colchester; St Nicholas No 257, Harwich; Perfect Friendship No 250, Chelmsford; and Freedom No 430, Maldon. The last two mentioned appear not to have been active and were erased from the list in 1782 and 1785 respectively.

Dunckerley inaugurated two new lodges, Unity which met at the King's Head, Headgate, Colchester, warranted 11 June 1776 and Social, which met at Braintree and was warranted on 9 June 1777. Both lodges attracted people of financial standing. The Lodge of Unity was erased in 1791.

There are no available minutes previous to 1837 but W Bro Keith S. Buck in a bicentenary history* in 1976 suggests that Dunckerley used the occasion of the constitution of the Lodge of Unity to appoint Thomas Boggis as his Deputy Provincial Grand Master, the Rev W. M. Leake as Provincial Grand Secretary and the Rev J. Firebrace as Provincial Grand Chaplain.

Boggis, a wealthy cloth merchant, held his appointment until his death in 1790. Leake was the first Master of the Lodge of Unity and subsequently became Provincial Grand Master of Gibraltar and Andalusia for two years from 1788.

The 1777 Provincial Grand Lodge was held at Chelmsford and the newspaper report tells us that several ladies honoured the Society with their company at a public breakfast after which

*History of Provincial Grand Lodge of Essex

83

they were permitted to see the regalia and form of the lodge and were addressed by the Provincial Grand Master. One lady was inspired to compose a poem 'To the Antient and Respectable Society of Freemasons' that very morning. The collection of £9 1s 6d at the church was given to the poor of the parish.

The Provincial Grand Lodge held on 12 August 1793 must have presented Chelmsford with one of its most impressive spectacles for many years. Over 100 brethren wearing regalia and 'cock' hats' marched in procession, mostly two by two, led by a band playing stirring martial music.

Carried in the procession were three 'great wax lights' in elegant and inlaid candlesticks 3 feet high. The *Book of Constitutions* and the Bible, each on a velvet cushion and covered with Royal blue silk, were carried by two Worshipful Masters.

Royal Arch companions wearing sashes and medals were in the procession as also were Knights Templar wearing black silk sashes ornamented with a silver star of five points, a cross of gold and an appendage of white satin.

Preceding the Provincial Grand Master was the Provincial Grand Sword Bearer and accompanying him were the Deputy Provincial Grand Master and Captain Sir William Hannam, acting Grand Master for England of the Knight Templar.

A hymn composed by Dunckerley was sung at the Church service.

After dinner the Lodge of Good Fellowship was constituted and Dunckerley gave address and, according to the *Freemasons' Magazine* . . .

> at an early hour the Provincial Grand Master took a most affection-
> ate leave of the brethren who with hearts full of fraternal esteem and
> cordial regard accompanied him, preceded by the band of music to
> the Black Boy and after giving him three hearty and heartfelt cheers
> parted with his amiable veteran who has been justly styled 'the great
> luminary of Masonry'.

It was a wonderful farewell for Dunckerley but probably not so pleasing for the neighbours of the Black Boy Inn who had retired for an early night!

21

LOYAL AND ROYAL DORSET

IT WAS NOT until 23 March 1783 that a patent was issued appointing Dunckerley Provincial Grand Master although he had been in control of the Province of Dorset as 'Superintendent of the Lodges' since 1777 and had been regarded as such.

The grand old Lodge of Amity No 137 which was warranted in 1765 and still meets at Poole, provides evidence of Dunckerley's activities, although their minutes, as was the custom in those days, are very scant. Little did they realise how interested the brethren of 200 years later would be!

The meeting of the lodge (then No 275) on 21 June 1780 was opened by the Provincial Grand Master. The reason for his attendance, it would seem, was to get the brethren together for two days later the lodge held an 'emergency for chosing officers on account of our R.W.P.G.M. holding a P.G. Lodge tomorrow', at Poole.

Tomorrow came and Dunckerley presided, supported by Dr Alexander Campbell, the Deputy Provincial Grand Master, and the following officers: John Leer, SGW; John Colbourne, JGW; John Starks, PG Treasurer; Bravill Friend, PG Secretary; the Rev George March, PG Chaplain; James Hamilton, PG Almoner; Joseph Rule, PG Std Bearer; 12 stewards and a visiting brother, Dr Thomas Jeans, Provincial Grand Warden of Hampshire.

Dunckerley, reporting to Grand Lodge on the second Provincial Grand Lodge at Poole on 12 August 1783, wrote

We embark'd in three Sloops, preceded by the Dorsetshire Band, and din'd by the Castle belonging to Mr. Sturt (Member for the County), where the flag was display'd and a royal salute was made from the Battery which we return'd with three time three.

In the evening Dunckerley attended a meeting of Amity Lodge at Poole and this is recorded in their minutes.

Lodge of Emergency. This night the Right Worshipf[l] Provincial Grad Master Brother Dunckerley Visited this Lodge, the day having been Spent in grand order and decorum by the Brethren on the Water wth Brother Dunkerley in honour of the Prince of Wales's Birth Day, who came of Age this day, and the Even[g] was concluded wth grand fire Works by Bro. Ford.

There were three visitors at the lodge, one being Van Dyke who painted Dunckerley's portrait.

The following evening there was another emergency meeting of Amity Lodge and two candidates – John Akerman and Richard Allen – were initiated by 'the R[t] Worshipful Provincial G[d] Master Bro. Dunkerly'.

Twenty years later Akerman, the captain of a British merchant ship, was captured by a French privateer off Portland and taken to France. It is recounted that as the Prize Master was examining the ship's papers he found Akerman's Grand Lodge certificate and immediately grasped his hand in fraternal greeting and conveyed to him that had he known he was a brother mason he would have put him ashore at Portland.

Unfortunately Akerman remained a prisoner of war for 11 years, but had the experience of having a Christmas dinner on the orders of Brother Napolean Bonaparte!

The last recorded occasion on which Dunckerley visited Dorset was 12 August 1791 when he held a Provincial Grand Lodge at Shaftesbury 'in honour of the birthday of our Royal Grand Master', the Prince of Wales, later King George IV.

Alexander Campbell, who had come from the north and opened a practice in the town as a surgeon and apothecary, is described by H. P. Smith in his *History of the Lodge of Amity No 137* (published in 1937) as the pioneer of freemasonry in Poole.

He and Dunckerley established a friendship of mutual respect and Dunckerley appointed him as his Deputy Grand Master of Dorset.

On 9 March 1787 Dunckerley wrote to inform Campbell that the previous day he had been presented to the Prince of Wales and added: 'His Royal Highness acquainted me with his intention of being a Royal Arch Mason, and I am to have the honour of being present at his exaltation. Present my affect^e greeting to all the brethren – Madam unites with me in sincere regard.'

The seafaring towns had an appeal for Dunckerley as an ex-naval man. Poole was the principal English port for trade with Newfoundland and the combination of circumstances retained in Dunckerley an interest for freemasonry in North America and Canada.

A warrant for a new lodge at Placentia was issued in 1784 and this led to a petition the following year for another lodge at Harbour Grace, as the following extract from a letter by Dunckerley to Grand Secretary White, written on 21 April 1785, shows.

> You may remember I jockey'd Dermot out of Newfoundland by obtaining a Warrant for a Lodge at Placentia, it has produced another petition for a Lodge. Harbour Grace on the Island, I rec'd it his morning under cover of a letter from my very worthy Deputy, Doctor Campbell of Pool. I beg you will get it executed (in the same neat manner as that for Gloucester) as soon as possible and send it (by the Pool Coach) to Alex. Campbell Esq., at that place, as the Ship that is to convey it is under sailing orders.

This was before the two rival Grand Lodges united in 1813. Dunckerley was aligned with the 'Moderns' and Laurence Dermott was the Deputy Grand Master of the rival 'Antient' or 'Athol' Grand Lodge and his 'victory' over Dermott obviously pleased him.

Provincial Grand Lodges were held by Dunckerley at Poole in 1780; Dorchester, 1781; Weymouth, 1783; Blandford, 1786; Shaftesbury, 1792; and Sherborne, 1793.

At the Blandford meeting Dunckerley recommended that lodges appointed their officers annually instead of every six months.

22

NO EASY PATH IN WILTSHIRE

As THE PROVINCIAL head of Wiltshire Dunckerley did not have a rose-strewn path and his skill as a diplomat and mediator was more then once put to the test.

The fund for building a hall for Grand Lodge was launched in 1768 and each lodge was expected to contribute 2s 6d for every initiate. By 1773 each lodge was ordered to send Grand Lodge a regular list of members with particulars of age, title, profession or trade and for every person made a Mason pay 5s, and 2s 6d for each person becoming a lodge member.

Many lodges felt they were so far removed from London their members might never even see the new London hall. The Salisbury Lodge in 1777 were building and furnishing a hall for themselves without outside help and felt Grand Lodge should do the same and Dunckerley had a busy period as mediator between them and Grand Lodge.

His efforts, however, were not unheeded for the Lodge expressed their thanks to him for his 'affectionate attention to the welfare of the Salisbury Lodge at the Quarterly Committee when they undeservedly were erased from the list for that glorious struggle which should render them doubly respectable in the esteem of all real Masons'.

The lodge later consented to pay 5s for every person initiated but denied 'the legality of this demand'. Dunckerley presided over the Provincial Gand Lodge at Salisbury in September 1777 and the Salisbury brethren paid 2 guineas for the hall and 1 guinea for the Fund of Charity.

There was also trouble with the Lodge which met at the

Crown Tavern at Devizes and Dunckerley complained to Grand Lodge in November 1777 that they had 'in a refactory manner' refused to correspond with him or give him any account of their situation.

His resolution that the lodge be informed that unless they acquiesced and attended to their duty they would be erased was carried. Grand Lodge expressed thanks to Dunckerley for his 'unwearied zeal'.

The most vicious opposition came from Sarum Lodge after they complained in 1781 that the appointment of Dunckerley to the 'superintendance' of Wiltshire was not formally notified to them and they wanted 'a person of consequence' as the provincial head.

Grand Lodge showed tact in dealing with a very delicate situation. To the Lodge the Grand Secretary (William White) wrote: 'The appointment of so worthy a brother who is not higher in Rank than Esteem in the Society cannot fail I apprehend of being satisfactory to you . . .' and asked them to set aside pique and trivial cavil,

He wrote assuring Duckerley that it was the wish of the Grand Lodge brethren to have everything made as agreeable to him as his endeavours for the prosperity of the Society so justly merited.

The Lodge continued to ignore Dunckerley.

In desperation Grand Lodge 'seeking some expedient of a mild and healing nature and not to proceed to extremities' asked Dunckerley 'as a favour . . . for the sake of harmony and peace and as farther proof of your forbearance and uniform inclination to promote every wish of the Fraternity' to resign the superintendence of Wiltshire 'without any kind of notice to the Sarum Lodge' and become the Provincial Grand Master of Somerset, an office which the Lodge of Virtue at Bath had requested him to accept.

This, it was suggested, would convey the highest degree of masonic respectability to Dunckerley and be an indirect rebuke to the Sarum Lodge. But the old warrior would not retreat and in effect replied that he should not be expected to resign because, of a lodge 'which was struck off the list for contumacious behaviour to the Grand Lodge but restored at my request'.

He had also acquired a house in Salisbury and intended to spend most of his time there.

'If it is the will of the Grand Lodge,' he wrote 'that the Sarum Lodge should continue on the list with the same contumacious disposition towards me, be it so! I shall never trouble Grand Lodge any more concerning them.'

Dunckerley remained as 'superintendent' and Sarum Lodge dealt direct with London and did not defect to the 'Antients', but after the death of Dunckerley further trouble with the lodge occurred and it was finally struck off in 1801.

23

BRISTOL AND GLOUCESTER

THE PROVINCE OF Gloucestershire was formed in 1753 when Sir Robert de Cornewall was appointed the Provincial Grand Master but he appears to have held the office in name only for there are no records of meetings on a provincial scale being held. The province then included the City of Bristol and was composed entirely of Bristol lodges.

Dunckerley was appointed Provincial Grand Master of Gloucestershire on 3 May 1784, and on 16 August 1784 he held the first recorded Provincial Grand Lodge of Gloucestershire at the Bush Tavern in Corn Street, Bristol.

At this meeting he intended appointing Brother Jasper Hawkins, Right Worshipful Master of the Lodge of Hospitality as the Provincial Grand Secretary, but as Hawkins had to go to sea, Brother Lewis was appointed in his place.

Brother Hopkins, RWM of the Beaufort Lodge, was

appointed Provincial Grand Treasurer.

Other appointments were Bro Joshua Springer, Provincial Grand Senior Warden, who later in the year became the Deputy Provincial Grand Master; Bro Maddicks, RWM of Jehosaphat Lodge, Provincial Grand Junior Warden; Bro Vaughan, Sword Bearer; and Bros M'Carthy, Wasborough, Maillard, Walters, Shortridge and Trotman, Stewards.

The Lodge started at 11 am and dinner was 'on the table' at 2 pm, the tickets for which were 5s each.

After this meeting Dunckerley sent the following contributions to Grand Lodge: Union Lodge No 253, Rising Sun, Bristol, £2 2s; Lodge of Jehosaphat No 359, White Hart, Bristol, £2 2s; Sea Captsins' Lodge, Three Tuns, Bristol, £3 12s. The last mentioned lodge was a forerunner of the Royal Sussex Lodge of Hospitality. He was determined to get the province on a business-like footing.

The first lodge in the Province of Gloucestershire came into existence on 10 January 1785 when Dunckerley sent a dispensation for the Royal Gloucester Lodge to be held at the Ball Inn in Gloucester. On his behalf the warrant was signed by Brother Springer as the Deputy Grand Master and was witnessed by Bro Jno. Carteret Lewis, as the Provincial Grand Secretary.

Dunckerley constituted the lodge at Gloucester in June 1785 and then went on to Bristol where he held a Provincial Grand Lodge for the County of Gloucester with the City and County of Bristol, at the Assembly Room in Princes Street on 24 June. A service was held at St Mary Redcliff Church.

THE CITY PROVINCE

It soon became clear to Dunckerley that Bristol, for better administration, should be a separate province and it was created in the latter part of the summer of 1786 with the boundaries corresponding to those of the City.

That this reorganisation would enable him to appoint more provincial officers and stewards would, said Dunckerley, 'be of great advantage to the Society, as it attracts the notice of the principal gentlemen in the several counties, who seem ambitious to attend me at my Provincial Grand Lodges'.

He was now (1786) in charge of seven Provinces and 29 lodges which were spread as follows – six in Bristol, four in Dorset, six in Essex, one in Gloucestershire, five in Hampshire, six in Somerset and one in the Isle of Wight.

He was also the Royal Arch Grand Superintendent of 18 counties. He was a busy man with a great deal of responsibility. He appointed Brother Springer to be the Deputy Provincial Grand Master of Bristol as well as of Gloucestershire.

And everything seemed to go well. On 21 November 1786 he reported to Grand Lodge.

> I have in the course of this year held Grand Lodges at Colchester, Blandford and Bristol. I was favor'd with the attendance of near two hundred Brethren (on His Majesty's Birthday) in Procession to the Church at Wells: and the Ladies honour'd us with their company at the Assembly Room: where, like the welcome Sun, at high twelve, they beautify'd, adorn'd, and enliven'd our happy meeting.

Dunckerley was not a remote Provincial Grand Master and his example provided the basis for the present system of provincial control. He liked to visit his lodges and often participated in the ceremonies. 'Instruction' was, he felt, a vital part of his duties.

There was an instance of this on 15 August 1789. He was present at the initiation of three candidates in the Royal Sussex Lodge of Hospitality and after the ceremonies he gave 'a most excellent charge'. Three days later at a meeting of the Lodge, called at 9.30 in the morning, he himself performed the initiation ceremony and delivered two lectures.

24

SOMERSET – APPOINTMENT BY ACCLAIM

ON 3 MAY 1784 Dunckerley received the dual appointment of Provincial Grand Master of Gloucestershire and Somerset.

His appointment to Somerset stemmed from a letter written to Grand Lodge by the Worshipful Master, Bro Henry Youngclass, of the Lodge of Virtue, Bath, more than a year before (on 6 February 1783).

The letter read

> We beg to inform the Grand Lodge we should be happy in having a Provincial Grand Master appointed for this County; we have petitioned our most worthy Bro Thos. Dunckerley Esq. to accept that office; he informs us the Grand Lodge will not permit him to preside over any more provinces than what he already holds. We should esteem it a particular favour of the Grand Lodge to nominate a Gentleman for us who lives in or near this County.

To this letter Grand Lodge replied

> In consequence of the desire intimated of having Bro. Dunckerley appointed as Prov. G.M. for your County our worthy Bro. Heseltine has wrote to him to know if he will accept of it (in which case another Gentleman will be appointed for Wiltshire) and as soon as we have an answer you shall be informed of it. You certainly could not have thought of a more worthy or better Mason than Bro. Dunckerley nor of one that is more zealous to promote the interest of the Craft.

At the time Dunckerley was living in Salisbury. On 25 March he wrote to the Grand Secretary:

I am much obliged to the Brethren of Bath for the regard they express for me, and should be happy to render them any service, but cannot prevail with myself to take Somersetshire and resign the County where I now reside and (with God's permission) propose to remain; and it would be ingratitude to the Lodge of Science in this City who have been at the expense of a Warrant of Constitution to be under my Authority and Instruction.

He was appointed Provincial Master of Somerset and, as we know, remained in charge of Wiltshire on a 'temporary' basis which lasted his lifetime.

As the head of Somerset he brought his personality and drive to bear without delay.

The first Provincial Grand Lodge was held on 19 August 1784 at the White Hart Inn, Stall Street, Bath. The *Bristol Journal* reported that the attendance was 'very numerous and respectable and the entertainment plentiful and elegant . . . the day was spent with that social harmony which has ever characterised the brotherhood and was indeed "The feast of reason and the flow of soul" '.

Dunckerley obviously appealed to the 'flow of the soul', for he sent to Grand Lodge another draught for £25 lent to the Hall Fund by the Rev Edmund Gardiner of Charles Street, Bath. He promised to send a report on the state of all the lodges under his care in October and hoped to send 'near £30 for the Charity and Hall Funds for several lodges'.

A postscript read 'Very bad pen and ink'. He would have been surprised to know that the letter would have been produced from United Grand Lodge archives and read with ease two centuries later.

Subsequent Provincial Grand Lodges were held at Wells. Reporting on this meeting in June 1786, the *Bath Journal* had this to say.

The appearance of the fraternity . . . was most numerous and respectable indeed. The procession to St. Cuthbert's Church, preceded by a band of wind music, was regular and splendid; the officers of the different Lodges with their jewels, the grand officers and standards in their appropriate clothing and several Reverend brothers dressed in their canonicals, made one of the grandest spectacles that have ever, perhaps, been seen in that part of the country.

An excellent dinner in every respect was provided by Brother Bacon; many masonic and loyal toasts were given, and the day concluded in order and harmony; it was indeed so well and so cheerfully conducted throughout the whole, that all were happy in the Lodge; and many poor and infirm brothers had all it rendered so by their donations.

The Festival of St John the Evangelist on 27 December 1784 was celebrated by the Provincial Grand Master and 120 brethren attended Bath Abbey Church where the Rev Bro Dart was the preacher and pointed out that freemasonry was founded on the devine principle of acting justly, loving mercy and walking humbly with God.

A hymn, written by Dunckerley, was sung by the choir and after the service the brethren returned in procession to the Bear Inn to spend the remainder of the day in 'festivity, harmony and fraternal affection'. Several petitions from distressed brethren were attended to.

Understandably Dunckerley had a great affection for the beautiful Roman city of Bath, and I am grateful to W Bro W. V. S. Smith, Archivist of the Royal Cumberland Lodge No 41 for the following:

The Royal Cumberland Lodge was originally known as The Bear Lodge for it met fortnightly at the Bear Inn in Cheap Street, Bath, on the site now occupied by a national firm of chemists. The Bear Lodge's deputation or charter dates from 1733 and bears the original seal of Grand Lodge. After more than 50 years as 'Lodge at the Bear Inn' the brethren found themselves in difficulties both as to numbers and finances. They must have heartily welcomed the suggestion of Provincial Grand Master Dunckerley that they amalgamate with the newly-founded Royal Cumberland Lodge No 458. This was carried into effect on 20 December 1785 when the Royal Cumberland Lodge members, its name, working, by-laws and furniture were transferred to the Bear Lodge which retained its own number 39. Among the articles transferred was a silver Hall

Medal.

There is a further record that at the union of the two lodges the Royal Cumberland mode of working which probably owed something to Dunckerley and a Brother William Finch, was adopted. In 1805, however, it was 'resolved to work the lecture used in the other Bath Lodges, which is an abridgment of that now used'.

Such is the manner in which tradition is lost!

Dunckerley's predecessor as Provincial Grand Master of Somerset was John Smith whose duties as Member of Parliament forced him to spend most of his time in London.

He was Master of the Royal Cumberland Lodge on several occasions but did not attend the lodge after June 1768 when his last term as Master ended. He died in London in November 1775 through 'bursting a blood vessel in a violent fit of coughing'.

In 1785 Dunckerley invested as his deputy Thomas West, apothecary of Bath.

One of Dunckerley's final acts at Provincial Grand Master of Somerset was to consecrate the Rural Philanthropic Lodge No 291 which still meets at Burnham-on-Sea. The Lodge was warranted by Dunckerley in the January of 1793 and the first meeting was held in the February but it was not consecrated until two years later.

Sixty-six signatures were appended to the original by-laws of the lodge and of these 38 are accompanied by a mark, although the majority are not monograms nor similar to those found on old buildings. S, possibly an allusion to Solomon, is the favourite and appears in triangles, circles and squares. H appears three times (a reference to Hiram?) and AB four times, each enclosed in various figures. J or I occur several times.

25

HIS LAST AND SMALLEST PROVINCE – HEREFORDSHIRE

DUNCKERLEY'S LAST appointment as Grand Master was to the Province of Herefordshire on 5 May 1790. It was also his smallest Province for there was then only one lodge, Palladian No 187. It was warranted in 1762 and is still working at Hereford as No 120, the oldest of the 14 lodges in the Province.

On 25 January 1791 Dunckerley constituted the Silurian Lodge No 576 at Kington. This seems to have ceased about the time of Dunckerley's death and ten years later the warrant was transferred to Ludlow, the name being changed to The Mercian Lodge but it was erased in 1832.

A Provincial Grand Lodge was held at the Bowling Green Inn, Hereford, on 12 August 1791 and was 'opened in ample form at 10 o'clock in the fore noon by Brother Dunckerley'.

At 11 o'clock the brethren processed to St Peter's Church for divine service. An anthem was sung by the Charity School children and a sermon was preached by the Grand Chaplain after which the brethren proceeded to the College Hall where the Provincial Grand Master delivered a charge.

It is recorded.

> An elegant dinner was served up, after which many loyal and Masonic toasts were drunk and the evening spent in the greatest harmony and several very good Masonic songs being sung the Lodge was closed at eight o'clock in ample form.

Among the 'near 150' who were present was 'His Grace Brother Charles Duke of Norfolk, who was the previous Provincial Grand Master.

The Royal Edward Lodge was opened at Leominster in November 1793. It was active up to 1814 when interest began to wane and it was erased 14 years later.

Grand Lodge, *November* 24, 1790.

THE Right Hon. *Lord* RAWDON, G.M. in the Chair, acquainted the Grand Lodge, that in confequence of the Death of His Royal Highnefs, the Duke of *Cumberland*, which, with the Society, his Lordfhip very much lamented, he had at the Inftance of the Grand Officers, taken the Senfe of His Royal Highnefs the *Prince of Wales*, as to his doing the Society the very high Honour of accepting the Office of Grand Mafter, and that it was with infinite Pleafure he could acquaint the Brethren, that His Royal Highnefs, had confented to accept of the Office, if elected thereto; whereupon His Lordfhip propofed *That His Royal Highnefs the* PRINCE *of* WALES, *be elected Grand Mafter of Mafons for the remainder of the Year,* which was feconded by Sir *Peter Parker*, Bart. D. G. M. and on the Queftion being put, it paffed *unanimoufly* in the *Affirmative,* and was accompanied by the moft animated demonftrations of Joy and Refpect.

Refolved, That Lord *Rawdon* and Sir *Peter Parker*, be requefted to wait upon His Royal Highnefs the *Prince of Wales*, to notify his Election to the Office of *Grand Mafter,* and to exprefs the moft grateful and dutiful Acknowledgments of the Grand Lodge to His Royal Highnefs, for affording his moft illuftrious Patronage and Protection to the Society.

Hampton Court Palace Dec 24 1790

My Dear Bro

I moft fincerely congratulate yourfelf and my Brethren at Bath on the Prince of Wales becoming our Grand Mafter. I beg you to acquaint the Knights Templars at Bath that feveral Encampments have requefted of one to accept the Office of Grand Mafter of that antient and noble Order I defire you will favour one with the names of thofe who approve of my acceptance of that Office, will be agreeable. To whom and all the Brethren, pleafe to prefent my moft affec Regards.

Your faithful Bro & &c Dunckerley

If — give one any more trouble — him to make his Appn to one.

Figure 9

A printed letter informing brethren that the Prince of Wales had been elected Grand Master of the Craft and to which Thomas Dunckerley has added his acceptance of becoming Grand Master for Knights Templar

26

GRAND MASTER OF THE KNIGHTS TEMPLAR

IT WOULD BE incorrect to claim that Dunckerley introduced Knights Templarism to this country.

Robert Freke Gould expresses the opinion that it had its origin in some form of the Scots Degree whence in all probability it penetrated into the British military lodges during or before the seven years war.

The purpose of this book, however, is not to trace the history of any degree but to recount the part played by Thomas Dunckerley, and it cannot be denied that he did more than anyone to promote its interests and to stimulate its growth.

He has been given the credit of making Knights Templar into the separate degree of the Royal Exalted Religious and Military Order of Knights Templar of St John of Jerusalem, but again it might be more correct to say he was one of those who was active in its formation as such.

As with the Royal Arch, the Knights Templar order was very close to his heart and his enthusiasm was rewarded when, in his own words, Dunckerley tells us. 'I was selected Grand Master to revive the Order in England in February 1791'.

The invitation originated from the brethren in Bristol. In a letter to the *York Knights Templar* in 1791 Dunckerley claimed '. . .Being Grand Superintendent at Bristol, I was requested by the Knights Templar in that city (who have had an Encampment time immemorial) to accept the office of Grand Master . . .'

The prospect of being Grand Master pleased him and those who had not expressed their support were given a gentle prompting as in this letter (see *Fig* 9) which was ostensibly to inform brethren that the Prince of Wales (later King George IV) had been elected Grand Master of the Craft. 'I beg you to acquaint the Knights Templar in Bath that several encampments have asked me to accept the Grand Mastership. I desire you will favour me with the names of those who approve my acceptance of that office . . .'

Dunckerley's first step as Grand Master was to set up a register of Encampments with the names, ages, professions and addresses of all the Knights. He then formed statutes for regulating the Order and appointed a Grand Encampment of All England.

The introductory sentence to the Statutes explained that the Knights Templar were animated by a desire to revive their order by the flourishing state of symbolic masonry, under the protection of His Royal Highness the Prince of Wales and the great increase of Royal Arch Chapters, patronised by the Duke of Clarence.

By the end of the year Dunckerley had constituted the following 11 Conclaves:

Observance of the Seven Degrees	London Coffee House, Ludgate Hill
Redemption	York
Royal Cumberland	Bear Inn, Bath
Fortitude	First Regiment of Dragoon Guards
Trine	New Ring of Bells, Bideford
Naval	Portsmouth
Durnovarian	Royal Oak, Dorchester
Harmony	White Hart, Salisbury
Science	Parade Coffee House, Salisbury
Royal Edward	Bowling Green, Hereford
St John of Jerusalem	Redruth

By 1794 there were 24 encampments.

A KNIGHTS' TEMPLAR HYMN

For all the Saints who from their labours rest,
Who Thee by faith before the world confess'd,
Thy name, O Jesu, be for ever blest.

Alleluia!

O may Thy soldiers, faithful, true and bold,
Fight as the Saints who nobly fought of old,
And win, with them, the victor's crown of gold.

Alleluia!

And when the strife is fierce, the warfare long,
Steals on the ear the distant triumph-song,
And hearts are brave again, and arms are strong.

Alleluia!

But lo! there breaks a yet more glorious day;
The Saints triumphant rise in bright array.
The King of glory passes on His way.

Alleluia!

From earth's wide bounds, from ocean's farthest coast,
Through gates of pearl streams in the countless host,
Singing to Father, Son and Holy Ghost.

Alleluia!

Figure 10
A Knights Templar hymn

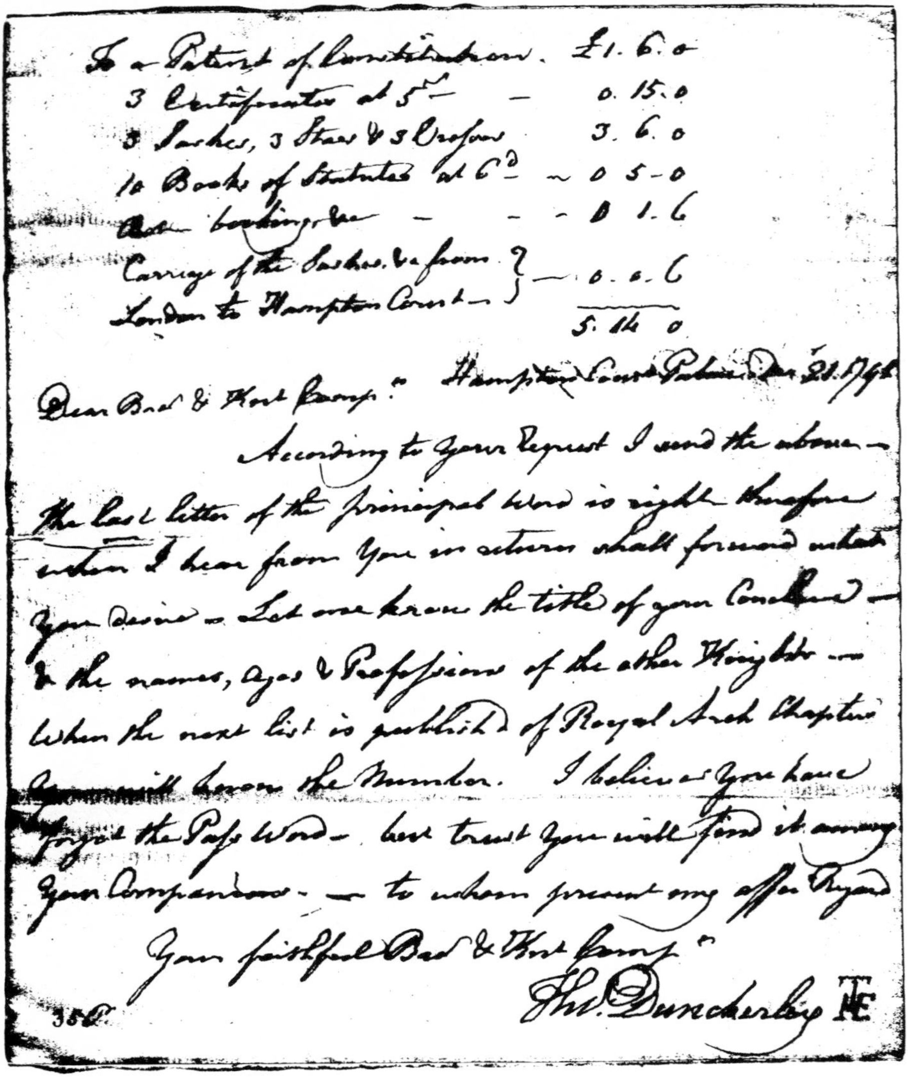

To a Patent of Constitution . £1. 6. 0
3 Certificates at 5ˢ — 0. 15. 0
3 Sashes, 3 Stars & 3 Crosses 3. 6. 0
10 Books of Statutes at 6ᵈ — 0 5 0
..... booking &c — — — 0 1. 6
Carriage of the Sashes &c from } — 0. 0. 6
London to Hampton Court — } ————
5. 14 0

Dear Bro & Most Excellt Compn: Hampton Court Palace Dec 21. 1795

According to your Request I send the above —
the last letter of the principal word is right therefore
when I hear from you in return shall forward what
you desire — Let me know the title of your Conclave —
& the names, Ages & Professions of the other Knights —
When the next list is publish'd of Royal Arch Chapters
..... will know the Number. I believe as you have
forgot the Pass Word — here trust you will find it among
your Companions. — to whom present my offers &c

Your faithful Bro & Most Excellt Compn:

Thos Dunckerley

Figure 11

Letter sent by Dunckerley to Druids Chapter of Love and Liberality, Redruth, giving the cost of establishing a Knights Templar Conclave. Dunckerley also gives a reminder about requiring the necessary passwords

Quebec, Novemb. 20*th,* 1793.

Dear Sir,

    I had the pleasure of being favoured with your kind letter of the 4th of July, about three weeks since ; accept of my thanks for your communication of the proceedings of the Grand Chapter. I regret much that, from the nature of my situation, there is no likelihood of my removing from hence till June or July, next year; and (even then) it is out of my power to say whether my lot will carry me back to England, or to another foreign station. I shall think myself particularly fortunate, when circumstances will permit my meeting the Knights, in Grand Chapter, in London : of this, I request, you will assure them, the first time that you assemble ; begging them to accept of my most hearty and best wishes for their welfare and prosperity. I shall be flattered with hearing from you from time to time; and particularly so, when you are able to inform me, of the good state of your health. Having nothing further to add, I beg, with the sincerest esteem, to subscribe myself,

        Your most devoted and obedient servant,

        EDWARD,

        Colonel of the Roy. Fusileers.

Thos. Dunckerley, Esq.

Figure 12
A letter written to Dunckerley by Prince Edward

When the three Principals of the Druids Chapter of Love and Liberality, Redruth, inquired the cost and steps necessary to obtain a warrant for a Knights Templar Conclave, Dunckerley answered by return – on 26 August 1791 – that the price of a patent was £1 6s with 5s for each Knight for whom a certificate would be issued. As for procedure he wrote: 'If there are three or more Knights among ye I will grant you a Patent if you can send me the first letter of the Pafs Word and last letter of the sacred word.'

There seems to have been a little difficulty over the passwords and Dunckerley gives a gentle jibe in the letter which is reproduced (*Fig* 11)

This letter is headed with an account for regalia sent to the Chapter and was written from Hampton Court on 21 December 1791. Using modern spelling it reads.

According to your request I send the above. The last letter of the principal word is right therefore when I hear from you in return shall forward what you desire. Let me know the title of your Conclave and the names, ages and professions of the other Knights. When the next list is published of Royal Arch Chapters you will know the number. I believe you have forgot the pass word but trust you will find it among your companions to whom present my affec. regards.

This original letter is one of several priceless letters in Dunckerley's handwriting which are preserved by the Coombe Library and is reproduced by kind permission of the Worshipful Master and Librarian of the Cornubian Lodge No 450 at Hayle as is the letter written by Prince Edward, Grand Master of the Knights Templar (*Fig* 12).

Fig 13 is the first part of another letter from the Coombe Library. It was written by Dunckerley on 27 January 1792 to John Knight of Redruth. It is headed with a reproduction of the plate used by Dunckerley on handwritten certificates. Underneath is the text 'T.P.K. Initium Sapientie Amor Domini' – Love of the Lord is the beginning of wisdom.

Dunckerley stresses the difficulties in travelling long distances and gives an indication of his enthusiasm for the Degree when he says

> I am concerned that there is so great a distance between us, as it
> would give me much pleasure to communicate to every Conclave
> that I have constituted, the Masonic knowledge which I have
> gleaned in Europe, America & Africa for forty years past.

There are also details of the uniforms he had established to be
worn by the conclaves.

> The coat will take 14 buttons – ten in front and four for the hips and
> skirts with two very small gilt buttons at the opening of each sleeve
> and a white Kerseymere Waistcoat and white French basket but-
> tons – with black breeches. A cheap suit of clothes that may be worn
> by men of all professions, and at any time. I paid the taylor £4 4. 0.
> for my coat and waistcoat. In all the Chapters cock'd Hats and
> Cockades are worn with Swords and black velvet Stocks. The
> Stocks, Cockades and Swords to be kept in a box at each Chapter.
> Most of the Knights (I have more than 120 registered) have already
> appeared in their uniforms; in compliance with my recommendation
> and request; and shall be happy to hear that you add to ye number if
> not attended with inconvenience.

When a request was made to him for 'proper Royal Arch
Masons aprons' for Knights Companions Dunckerley explained
(August 1792): 'Royal Arch aprons were directed to be worn by
the old Charter, but have been disused for several years, Sashes
being deemed sufficient.'

At the end of his letter Dunckerley instructs John Knight in
the difference between the signature of the Knights Templar
and that of the Holy Royal Arch. He explains that the former,
Temple Hierosolymæ Eques is different from the Royal Arch
which is *Templum Hierosolymæ)*

That for the Knights Templar represents Knight of the Temple of Jerusalem and that for the Royal Arch, Temple of
Jerusalem.

In a preface to the *History of Freemasonry in West Cornwall
from 1765 to 1828* by J. G. Osborn, which was published in
1901, the historian W. J. Hughan refers to the elaborate design

Hampton Court
Palace

Jan.y 27th 1792

Dear Br & Knt Compn.n Sir John Knight.

Your Letter (Date unknown) I recd the 25th with a Draught for £3.14.0; which I immediately put in my Bureau — but lost the Letter the same day. However I wrote to Tower for the Sashes, &c but cannot remember the names of Your two Brother Knights; but have sent the Blank Certificates to be fill'd up. I have also left a Blank for the Day on which Your first Conclave is to be held. I am concern'd that there is so great a Distance between us: as it would give me much pleasure to communicate to every Conclave that I have constituted, the Masonic Knowledge which I have glean'd in Europe, America & Africa, for forty Years past.

Altho' Mrs Dunckerley (the Lady Patroness of Knt Templars) is near 80 Years of age, & I am not far from 70 — Yet we intend (with God's permission) to visit the West of England next Summer and (if we should winter at Plymouth) It is probable that I may have the happiness of conversing with some of the Knt Compns from Exeter, Redruth, & Biddeford.

Figure 13
The first page of a letter written by Dunckerley and addressed to 'Sir John Knight, Eminent Deputy Grand Master of the Conclave and Chapter of the Order of Knights Templars &c at Redruth Cornwall'. Dunckerley's seal in red wax was attached

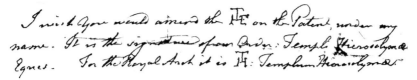

Figure 14
Extract from a letter Dunckerley wrote to John Knight where he explains
the difference between signatures for Knights Templar and Holy Royal
Arch

---

used on the old Knights Templar certificates.
He wrote

The 'M 1118' at the foot of the ladder, and N at the top, refer to
Masonry, and the Rose Croix, or Ne Plus Ultra, being the 'perfec-
tion of the Craft'. The letter M stands for the true basis on which all
the Degrees rest, the members being required to be just, upright,
and free men, of mature age, sound judgment, strict morals, and
believers in God, the Grand Architect of the Universe. The date
1118 refers to the year of origin of the K.T. The 11th. March 1314
witnessed the martyrdom of Jacques De Molay, Grand Master,
indicated by 'J.D.M.'
The Anno Ordinis (A.O.) is obtained by deducting 1118, and the
Anna Cœdis (A.C.) by substracting 1314 from the current years.
The Seven Steps allude to that number of Degrees included in the
Templar Rite, and the figures 3 to 81 are Masonic Numbers, begin-
ning with the 3, the supposed age of an Apprentice to the Square of
Nine, the completion of the System. With this explanation the
Certificate will also be understood as respects most of its symbolism.

Anno Ordinis is year of origin. Anno Cœdis is Year of slaughter.

Bro John Knight gave the following as the origin of the
hieroglyphical ladder.

As a Ladder, it is composed of two Sides and Seven Steps or

rounds. The two sides allude Philip the Fair, King of France, and Bertram Got Archbishop of Bordeaux; The Seven Steps allude to the 7 Conditions that Philip imposed on the Archbishop in case he got him elected to the Pontifical Chair, which the King Effected; and he took the title of Pope Clement the Sixth. Six of those conditions were but of little import, but the Seventh the King did not communicate to him till it was ripe for Execution, but he bound the Archbishop upon his Oath that he would fulfil it whenever the King should make his request: As a pledge of which they divided a heart, and each Kept a part to be a Witness for fulfilling his said Oath; which was to be the Total exterpation of the Knights Templars throughout Christendom in one Day which was fulfilled on the 11th March A.D. 1314.

Writing to Dunckerley on 18 February 1792 Knight, who the following year was appointed Provincial Grand Master of Knights Templar for Cornwall, reported

> I am informed that the Chapter at the Peace and Fame, Plymouth Dock, do make it a practise of Installing Knight Templars without any Patent whatever for so doing, and have very lately installed a Bro Companion of our Royal Arch Chapter.
>
> However, we are determined neither to admit him or any other person into our Conclave who is not regularly installed and registered under a Patent from your Grand Conclave. You will be so good as not to take any notice of this information as coming from me, as we are on a friendly footing as Brother Companion of the Royal Arch.

From the last sentence one can imagine that Knight felt as a schoolboy 'sneaking' to the headmaster on his comrades.

Dunckerley's only comment to Knight was 'I thank you for the hint "Peace and Fame" '.

27

A CALL TO ARMS

THE MOST REMARKABLE letter ever written by a Grand Master was printed by Dunckerley on 11 March 1794 and circulated to all the Knights Templar encampments under his control.

It called on all Knights Templar to join their county regiments to help guard the country from a threatened invasion by the French.

But Dunckerley, not the type of man to ask others to do what he was not prepared to do himself, and although then not in good health and in his 70th year, wrote: 'When the important moment arrives, I shall offer my service in the Navy or Army.'

Acknowledging the letter, John Knight wrote from Redruth.

Most Eminent and Supreme Grand Master

Agreeable to your desire, signified to me by your esteemed favour of the 11th. ultimo, I held a conclave of the Order of Knights Templars in our field of encampment at this place, on Monday the 28th. ultimo; where I laid your letter before the Knights Companions. – I have the happiness to inform you that I found them stedfast in their religious principles, and unanimous in their loyalty and patriotism to their King and Country. Two of the Knights Companions are officers in the Penryn Volunteers corps, and will follow your directions in wearing the Crofs of the Order, &c. – The rest of the Companions residing at a distance from any established corps, will be ready on an emergent occasion to unite with them; and they have entered into a subscription (as Knights Templars), to be applied

Emminent

Dear Brother and Eminent Knight Companion,

As the Nation is preparing to guard against an Invasion from our Enemies, if they should have the temerity to make an attempt, it is become my duty, at this important crisis, to request and require that such of you as can, without prejudice to your families, do hold yourselves in readiness (as Knights Templars) to unite with and be under the command of the officers of the military corps stationed in your respective counties, as may be most convenient, taking the name of 'Prince Edward's Royal Volunteers.' When the important moment arrives, I shall offer my service in the Navy or Army; and, whenever I have the honor to be received, shall inform you of my address; and although we are prevented, by adverse circumstances, from assembling together where I might have had the honor and happiness of commanding in person, yet our hearts will be united in the glorious cause, in conformity to the sacred obligations we are under. Let our prayers be addressed to the Throne of grace; that as Christ's faithful soldiers and servants we may be enabled to defend the Christian religion, our gracious Sovereign, our laws, liberties and properties, against a rapacious enemy. Let the word of the day be The will of God: *and let us remember, that a day, an hour of virtuous liberty, is worth a whole eternity of bondage.*

The Knights Companions are required to wear the uniform of the corps in which they serve as volunteers, with the Cross of the order of the Knights Templars on a black riband between two button-holes on the breast of the waistcoat.

It is my desire that you cause this letter to be read at the next meeting of your Chapter, and that they may be informed of my intention to hold the Annual Grand Conclave at the London Coffee-house, Ludgate-hill, on Sunday the 11th of next month, at two in the afternoon; dinner to be on table precisely at three o'clock, and the Conclave closed at six in the evening. From a consideration that it may be more convenient for the noble Knights who attend the Grand Feast at Free-Masons'-Hall on the 7th of next month, I have made the above alteration of our annual meeting. I shall breakfast at Nandoe's Coffee-house, near the Temple gate, on Sunday the 11th of May, at nine in the morning; where I shall be happy to meet those Knights Companions who can with convenience attend divine service in the Temple church at ten o'clock.

Your faithful Brother and Knight Companion,

Thomas Dunckerley. (*G. M.*)

Southampton, March 11th,
A.D. 1794, A.O. 676.

Figure 15
Dunckerley's letter calling on all Knights Templar to join their country and
help guard against a threatened invasion by the French in 1794

towards the defence of the country; and as there is a general subscription at Bodmin, for the county, and several volunteer corps on
the coast for local defence, we beg your opinion and advice how to
apply the money we have subscribed. I am (M.E. & S.G.M)

Your faithful and affect. Brother and Knight Companion

Redruth, 3rd. May 1794   J— K——

Dunckerley's reply was

Yesterday I read (with much pleasure) your favour of the 3rd. inst.
which shall be read next Sunday in the Grand Chapter. I honour the
patriotic and loyal spirit of your Chapter on the present occasion. It
is my humble opinion that it will be most eligible to pay your
subscriptions to the Treasurer of your County Meeting, in the name
of the Conclave of Knights Templars of St. John of Jerusalem, at
Redruth. You will hear from me soon with an account of the Grand
Chapter. In your next favor me with a list of your Royal Arch
Chapter. My affect. Greeting to the noble Knights from your faithful
Bro. &c.

The Knights Templar Grand Chapter was normally held on a
Sunday at the Surrey Tavern, Surrey Street, Strand, London,
preceded in the morning by attendance at divine service at the
Temple Church. The Conclave was opened at 2 pm, dinner was
served at 3 pm, and Conclave closed at 7 pm.

The call to arms was not confined to the Knights Templar as is
shown by a report in the *London Evening Post* of 19 August
1794 of a gathering of freemasons in London to celebrate the
birthday of the Duke of York.

The report said the occasion was

celebrated with all the Honours of Masonry by the Order of Knights
Templars resident at London, united with the Society of Antient
Masons of the Diluvian Order, or Royal Ark, and Mark Mariners,
assembled at the Surrey Tavern in the Strand, by Summons from
Thomas Dunckerley, Esq. Grand Master, and Grand Commander
of these united Orders.

DEAR SIR,   HALIFAX, July 19th. 1795.

I was favored on the 30th. of laſt month with your obliging letter of the 17th of April; for which, and the aſſurance therein contained of the kind remembrance of the Noble Knights, I beg to return you and them my moſt hearty thanks. It gives me the trueſt ſatisfaction to hear that the order increaſes ſo rapidly; and I am particularly pleaſed to learn from you, that the zeal of the Knights has induced thoſe reſiding in Cumberland, Cornwall and the diſtant Counties, to enroll themſelves in the regiments ſtationed in thoſe counties; I think your own intention of ſtanding forward in defence of the Kingdom highly meritorious. I was much concerned to bear of your having ſuffered ſo much from ill health; but ſincerely hope, as your letter is written in moſt excellent ſpirits, that you are thoroughly recovered. It remains for me to return you my thanks for the very polite attention you paid to the celebration of my Birth-Day and to requeſt, that you will aſſure the Noble Knights of my particular friendly remembrance; truſting that you will remain aſſured, that I ſhall ever be proud to acknowledge myſelf,

Your truly devoted and obedient,

Humble Servant,

To THOMAS DUNCKERLEY, Esq.

HAMPTON COURT PLACE,

MIDDLESEX.

EDWARD.

MAJOR GENERAL, commanding His Majesty's Forces in the Province of Nova-Scotia, and its Dependencies.

Figure 16
Prince Edward's reply to Dunckerley's 'call to arms' letter

The United Orders unanimously resolved that they would provide themselves with arms and accoutrements, in order to 'defend this country against the Enemies of our happy Constitution'.

The report also establishes Dunckerley's status with the other degrees.

Prince Edward who was the Patron of these Orders was sent regular progress reports by Dunckerley expressed his approval of the letter and pleasure at the response it had received.

Writing from Halifax where he was stationed as a Major-General, the Prince wrote: 'I have only Time to return you my Thanks for the Communication of the very respectable Conduct of the Knights on the late Appearance of the French threatening to invade England; and I beg you to assure them the true Pleasure I have received from this Circumstance. His Majesty has decided for the present, that I shall remain to command in Nova-Scotia.'

This letter was dated 23 August 1794. In the July of the following year the Prince wrote (see *Fig* 16)

> It gives me the trueft satisfaction to hear that the order increafes fo rapidly; and I am particularly pleafed to learn from you, that the zeal of the Knights has induced thofe refident in Cumberland, Cornwall and the diftant Counties, to enroll themfelves in the regiments ftationed in thofe counties; I think your own intention of ftanding forward in defence of the Kingdom highly meritorious. I was much concerned to hear of your having fuffered fo much from ill health; but fincerely hope, as your letter is written in moft excellent spirits, that you are thoroughly recovered . . .

The Prince, whose daughter later became Queen Victoria, succeeding her uncle to the throne, was a serving soldier. As a Colonel in the Royal Fusiliers he was at Quebec in 1793 and then left Canada for the West Indies and was Major-General in command at Nova Scotia, and as soon as the campaign was over he returned to Halifax.

He was initiated in the Union Lodge in Geneva and the Grand Lodge in London bestowed on him the rank of Past Grand

Master. By patent 11 January 1790 he was appointed Provincial Grand Master for the garrison, town and territory of Gibraltar, and the Province of Andalusia in Old Spain. This was followed by appointment as Provincial Grand Master for Lower Canada in 1792. His part in bringing about the union of the rival Grand Lodges in 1813 is, of course, well known.

His letters to Dunckerley reveal an unflagging interest in freemasonry in Britain and particularly in the Knights Templar Degree. In a letter on 20 November 1793 he said he would think himself particularly fortunate when circumstances permitted him to meet the Knights in Grand Chapter in London.

Dunckerley's 'call to arms' letter (*Fig* 15) has been preserved in the Coombe Library and it is reproduced by courtesy of the Worshipful Master and Librarian of the Cornubian Lodge No 450, who also gave permission for the reproduction of the self-explanatory letter (*Fig* 16) from Prince Edward.

Two Knights Templar Songs

Dunckerley issued the following as the canticle for the Knights Templar:

> Hail! to the Royal band
> Who grace this happy land
> With valient Knights.
> May the United Three
> Of the Blessed Trinity
> Cement the Unity
>   Of Noble Knights

Twelve once were highly lov'd,
But one a traitor prov'd,
Put out his fire.
May Cymon haunt all fools
Who vary from our rules;
May the hearts of such fools
Rest high in Spire.
'Gainst Infidels we fight
And for religion's right,
We'll breathe our last.
Poor Pilgrims begging we
Will our Jerusalem see,
Manfully past.

It was sent to the Redruth Conclave in 1792 by the Bideford Conclave on Dunckerley's instructions but it is not stated that he wrote it, although he could well have done. Only the year before he had said that he knew of no hymns or odes for the Order but with God's assistance would attempt to compose one. He had already written a hymn to be sung after the opening of a Royal Arch Chapter.

He certainly wrote the next song and it was published in 1794 and it was credited to him.

At the bright temple's awful dome,
Where Christian knights in arms are drest;
To that most sacred place we come,
With cross and star upon the breast;
Pilgrims inspir'd with zealous flame,
Through rugged ways and dangers past;
Our sandals torn, our feet were lame,
But faith and hope o'ercame at last.

Remember, knights, the noble cause,
Let Simon's fate prevent your fall;
Be firm and true, obey the last,
Nor let the cock unheeded call.
Let none the sacred word profane,
Nor e'er, like Peter, Christ deny;
Your conduct still preserve from blame,
Nor let the urn be plac'd on high.

Unite your hearts, unite each hand,
In friendship, harmony, and love;
Connected thus Knights Templar stand,
Our love and charity to prove.
Until that awful final day
When fire shall melt this earthly ball,
Your courage and your faith display;
Attend to freedom's sacred call;

True to our God, our Laws, and King,
Devout, obedient, loyal, free.
The praise of royal Edward sing,
The patron of our mystery.
In uniform each knight is drest,
Distinguish'd all by black, red, blue,
The cross and star upon the breast,
Adorn the heart that's just and true.

If all the social Virtues of the Mind,
If an extensive Love to all Mankind,
If hospitable Welcome to a Guest.
And Speedy Charity to the Distrest,
If due regard to Liberty and Laws,
Zeal for our King and for our Country's cause,
If these are Principles deserving Fame,
Let Masons then enjoy the Praise they claim.

28

MASONIC COMPASSION AND CHARITY

BY NO MEANS was Dunckerley a wealthy man, but where charity was concerned he led by example.

An anonymous writer in the *Freemasons' Magazine* in 1842 probably correctly assessed him as a man of charity and masonic compassion when he wrote

> He was generous and hospitable to a fault; he gave Masonic parties very frequently at Hampton Court and was a constant attendant at all public meetings and festivals of the Craft. A poor and needy brother never applied to him in vain. The numerous claims on his time in so many provinces were so costly for his means that it will not be wondered at that he was himself always comparatively poor.

He was a friend and ardent supporter of Bartholomew Ruspini who conceived the idea of founding the Royal Cumberland Freemasons School, now universally known as the Royal Masonic Institution for Girls.

The oldest of the English masonic benevolent institutions, its inauguration on 25 March 1788 was a display of practical help and charity to the individual at a time when this was most needed.

The scheme was inaugurated on 25 March 1788 and Dunckerley was one of the select committee of eight elected to put it into operation and to acquire suitable premises. Five of the others, like him, were members of the Prince of Wales Lodge No 259.

The first schoolhouse was in Somers Place East. Now disappeared, it was between the present Euston and St Pancras railway stations.

On 5 January 1789 the doors were opened to 15 little girls who were committed to the care of the matron. They were awakened by a bell at 6 am in the summer months and at 8 o'clock on winter mornings.

An hour later they had breakfast of rice milk, water gruel or milk porridge. With their substantial mid-day dinner they had beer and again for supper which comprised bread and butter, bread and cheese or broth and bread. It is somewhat horrifying to think of five-year-olds drinking beer, but in those far-off days there were different standards and it was, I suppose, one way of supplementing their sugar intake.

Dunckerley took a great interest in the school and the little ones who, but for the institution, would have suffered much greater hardships.

At Provincial Lodges he recommended the brethren to give the school their support and to strengthen an impassioned plea at Chelmsford in 1793 he took out his purse and immediately subscribed £21, which was a considerable sum of money in those days and would even do credit to many brethren today.

This example was followed by every brother present making a contribution to the utmost of his means and a useful amount was raised.

No Grand Lodge was held in any of Dunckerley's provinces without a collection being taken for distribution to the needy, whether a brother, widow or the poor of the parish.

In the provinces Dunckerley was certainly as persistent as anyone in his efforts to raise money for the provision of a hall for Grand Lodge and its subsequent maintenance. His endeavours contributed to a large extent to Grand Lodge being able to acquire in 1774 the freehold of a house and a large garden in Great Queen Street and it is on this site that the present temple stands.

His insistence on lodges supporting the hall and charity funds is shown in this sentence from a letter he wrote to the Grand Secretary from Southampton in July 1784. 'If the lodge at Malden doth not contribute to ye hall and charity very soon I shall desire they may be struck off the list.' In other words a lodge which was not prepared to meet its obligations was not worthy of recognition.

He also asked when the lodge at Bridgwater contributed 'as I expect to meet them at Bath next month'. It sounded rather threatening. If they had not contributed Dunckerley intended to stir them from their lethargy!

On 31 January 1786 he sent Grand Lodge £25 as a loan to the Freemasons Hall from the Lodge of Liberty and Sincerity, Bridgwater. It was one of the lodges entitled to the Freemasons Hall medal. Unfortunately it was erased 5 March 1828. However, another great lodge of the Dunckerley era, Perpetual Friendship No 135, warranted 1764, still flourishes in this Somerset town.

On 21 July 1785 he informed Grand Lodge that the Royal Cumberland Lodge at Bath were ready to subscribe £25 to the Hall Fund and asked that a medal for them be sent to him at Hampton Court.

He intended to present it in person and it is a matter of great interest that this medal, almost 200 years later, hangs from the Square on the Worshipful Master's collar. It bears the original number of the lodge – 458. What a wonderful link with the past and with the efforts of Thomas Dunckerley.

Twenty-six lodges were awarded medals and the Bath brethren believe that their medal is the only original one left in the provinces.

This grand old lodge, of which Dunckerley was so proud, and which he loved to visit, is still working at Bath and has the number 41.

If only Dunckerley could walk along Great Queen Street and see the majestic building which is the shrine of Freemasons the world over. If only he could see the masonic activity which emanates from the Hall! He would be reassured that his untiring efforts were not in vain.

If only he could see the School at Rickmansworth with its boarders and day pupils, in all 477 girls, and know that Her Majesty the Queen is the Grand Patron.

There are also another 250 girls who are receiving grants for education other than in the School.

What a wonderful foundation was laid in 1788.

29

THE GREAT ENIGMA

NEARLY 260 YEARS have passed since Thomas Dunckerley was born and the claim that he was the natural son of the Prince of Wales who became King George II will never be established beyond all manner of doubt.

The claim put forward by Dunckerley centres around the poignant death-bed statement of his mother, and he obtained that second hand from her neighbour and confidante. If the occasion had arisen it would not have convinced a court of inquiry.

There are now just a few rare and valuable letters and certain circumstantial evidence which can be submitted in favour of the claim which, understandably, was never acknowledged or denied by the royal court.

Dunckerley adopted an armorial seal, engraved within a shield and border, bearing a baton sinister argent, reserved for illegitmate children of royalty, quartered by the Welsh harp and the lions of England and Scotland, contained in the Royal Arms of George II and surmounted by the royal crest. The seal bore an appropriate motto 'Fato Non Merito' – By Fate Not Desert.

Underneath was the name 'Thoˢ Dunckerley Fitz George'. The prefix 'Fitz' means son of and was used especially by the illegitimate sons of kings and princes. There could be no plainer or defiant way of telling the world that he was the son of a king.

In the few masonic references to these seals it has hitherto been said that permission to use them was granted by Royal Licence.

This is open to doubt. The Windsor Herald of the College of Arms has searched the official registers but can find no trace of a

Figure 17
The Arms assumed by Dunckerley. The baton across the shield is an
indication of illegitimacy

Figure 18
Various seals used by Thomas Dunckerley including his Coat of Arms
which has the prefix 'Fitz', meaning son, and which was used by the
illegitimate sons of Kings and Princes

grant or confirmation of arms to Thomas Dunckerley, either in the usual manner or by way of Royal Licence.

Neither can information be offered by his colleague, J. P. Brooke-Little, Norroy and Ulster King of Arms, who is preparing a book on Royal Bastards.

The College of Arms are the authority, possessing records which are complete and impartial, which leaves us with the query: Did Dunckerley blatantly assume arms with the baton sinister signifying he was of royal descent? It is kinder to think that he was given verbal permission.

The King was not a freemason but Dunckerley's masonic connections with royalty were extensive. Indication of this is given in casual references in some of his letters such as (on 10 August 1793) 'I had the honour of waiting on the Prince of Wales at Brighton'.

He was a close friend of Prince William Henry, Duke of Clarence, the third son of George III and of Prince Edward, the fourth son.

He used the seal openly and frequently and without let of hindrance from official quarters.

He also had another book plate with a completely different armorial and the Latin motto 'Honestas et Fortitude' – Honesty and Courage – which had been his guideline since he had adopted it when a child.

He had also a paper stamp which contained various masonic emblems within a circle but such stamps were not at this time unique.

The news that he was the son of the King must have been a great shock to Dunckerley whose naval rank of Gunner was far removed from court circles. He would certainly have needed time and advice, and he would not, as some seem to think he should have, make his new-found knowledge public. He lived in a period when national peace was subservient to international conflict and any delay in taking action is explained in his own statement.

The information gave me great surprise and much uneasiness and as I was obliged to return immediately to my duty on board the

Vanguard, I made it known to no person at that time but Captain Swanton . . . We were then bound a second time to Quebec, and Captain Swanton did promise me that on our return to England he would endeavour to get me introduced to the King, and that he would give me a character; but, when we came back to England, the King was dead.

I have flattered myself that my case would be laid before the King, and that I should have the honour and happiness to be presented to my royal master and father; and that his majesty, on recollecting the several circumstances, would have granted me an appointment equal to my birth; but, by the demise of my most gracious sovereign, my expectations were frustrated, and all my hopes subsided.

There were several influential persons who were sufficiently acquainted with what had happened to have the confidence to put Dunckerley's case before the King – the grandson of George II. A pension was awarded, but no reason was given.

Among the circumstantial evidence to support the claim is that Mary was conveniently married to cover any eventuality and then, after the baby was born and she was deserted by her husband she was allowed to remain at the Somerset House apartment which later passed to her son. She also received an annual bounty. Would, in normal circumstances, a woman deserted by her husband, be so favoured?

The interest taken in Mary during her pregnancy by those closely associated with the court suggests it was not just a case of an ordinary woman who had gone astray.

Mrs Cannon who delivered the baby was a well-known midwife of that period. She was the midwife at the birth in 1737 of Princess Augusta, the first child of the Princess of Wales who was the daughter-in-law of King George II. She lived in expensive Jermyn Street, St James's. She died on 11 December 1754, over five years before Mary.

The fees of Dr Richard Mead, MD, would most certainly have been beyond the means of Mary. His reputation at the royal court made him the most prominent physician of the period. It was recorded by a diarist of the time that in December 1717 he 'recovered the Princess of Wales when the other physicians would have killed her had their prescriptions been followed'.

Dr Mead also prescribed for the Walpoles and was appointed physician to King George II when he came to the throne in 1727 but had attended the King and Queen Caroline when they were Prince and Princess of Wales. He, too, died in 1754.

Then there was the £50 – a considerable amount of money in those days – sent to Mary by command of the Prince.

To me, Mary's statement rings true. She was probably a companion to Lady Walpole rather than a servant maid although it is doubtful if her father, Bolness, was qualified as a physician for there is no trace of him in any of the records or reference books held by the Royal College of Physicians.

Unfortunately nowhere is the Christian name given of 'Mr' Dunckerley, Mary's husband. Reference to the Royal Archives at Windsor Castle suggests it could have been Adam for there was a porter bearing that name at Somerset House from 1714.

This information comes from the Lord Steward's Papers for the period. Strengthening the theory of Mr Dunckerley's identity is the fact that the Duke of Devonshire's court appointments included that of Lord Steward of the Royal Household, and it is recorded by Mary that her husband went to Chatsworth on business for the Duke.

Unfortunately documentation of the early eighteenth century is rather scant in the archives held by the trustees of the Chatsworth Settlement and a search of all the sources available brought nothing to light regarding Mr Dunckerley.

Adam Dunckerley's successor at Somerset House on 15 January 1728 was a John Meaking who had been night porter there from 1715. The 'Mrs Meeking' mentioned by Mary in her deathbed statement was more than likely either the wife or a relative of John. Slight variations in the spelling of proper names was quite common in these days as seen from surviving letters.

All this ties up so well that it places Adam Dunckerley as Mary's husband and the legal father of Thomas beyond mere speculation.

Figure 19
A portrait of King George II to whom Thomas Dunckerley is said to have
borne a striking resemblance

30

PORTRAITS OF DUNCKERLEY

REPRODUCED IS A portrait of King George II who, according to Mary Dunckerley, was the father of Thomas (see *Fig* 19). There are two engravings of Thomas Dunckerley taken from oil paintings, one by Thomas Beach (*Fig* 20) and the second by P. Van Dyke (*Fig* 21) both of which are still extant, whilst a 'Van Dyke' portrait bought by Hospitality Lodge No 248 in 1808 was destroyed in the Second World War.

Thomas Beach did his portrait in 1787. It is 4 feet 2 inches deep and 3 feet 4 inches wide. The coat, waistcoat and cravat are of the period and the masonic regalia is a feature of the painting showing the collar and emblem of a Provincial Grand Master and a Royal Arch jewel on the left breast. It is from this painting that J. Jones made his engraving in 1789.

The oil painting (see frontispiece) hangs in the refectory of Loyal Lodge No 251 at Barnstaple in north Devon and from it the light brown eyes of Dunckerley seem to be focused directly down the long room towards the Worshipful Master as he sits at the head of the festive board. One has the feeling that the spirit of Dunckerley, who cherished the ritual masonry and the fellowship of the festive board, is present.

Although he was then not a mason, Beach presented his painting to the Royal Cumberland Lodge at Bath and it was acquired by members of Loyal Lodge when they bought their beautiful masonic Regency furniture from Brother Charles Geary of Bath in 1843, but that is another story.

Soon after the Second World War, and long before inflation raised its head, Loyal Lodge refused an opportunity to sell the painting for £1,000.

Figure 20
An engraving of Dunckerley by J. Jones taken from the portrait painted by
Thomas Beach in 1787 (*see frontispiece*)

The half-length portrait (*Fig* 21) in oils by 'Van Dyke' measures 28 inches by 24 inches and was bought by the Lodge of Amity No 137 in 1783 for £5 5s and the frame cost a princely 3s 6d (17½p)! It still has pride of place in the lodge and shows Dunckerley wearing a white court wig, lace cravat, red coat and white waistcoat, and masonic regalia is also a feature. An engraving of this portrait was made by C. West and published in 1786.

The Beach portrait is described in the Royal Cumberland Lodge minute book as 'excellent' which suggests that apart from artistic merit it was a true likeness. Of the Van Dyke portrait Dunckerley wrote, 'It is considered a good likeness'. On that comment we can put our own interpretation. An admirable copy in miniature of the Bèach portrait painted by Brother J. H. Groves, assistant curator, is exhibited at the Museum in Freemasons' Hall, Great Queen Street, London, and should give pleasure to all Dunckerley admirers.

On the gilt frame of the painting at the Lodge of Amity, there is an inscription which reads, 'Thos. Dunckerley, Grand Superintendent of the R.A.M. and Provincial Grand Master of Dorsetshire. Painted by Philip Van Dyke AL 5785 AD 1785'.

This gives rise to two queries. The difference between AL and AD is 4004 although the four was, and still is, often overlooked. If the former date is correct the Anno Domini should read 1781. The minutes of the lodge record payment for the painting under the date September 1783. W Bro J. W. Longhurst, the present lodge secretary, offers the suggestion that payment could have been made when the painting was commissioned and the work took two years.

Like the inscription, various sources credit Philip Van Dyke with the work but research suggests it is more likely the work of Peter Vandyke. Both were portrait painters of acknowledged ability but at the time Philip was more universally known. But Philip, who lived and worked in Amsterdam, was born on 10 January 1680 and died at the Hague on 3 February 1752/3 when Dunckerley was not even a mason and long before he became a Provincial Grand Master.

All the authoritative dictionaries on painters and engravers

Figure 21
The engraving of Dunckerley by C. West taken from an oil painting by P.
Van Dyke now hangs in the lodge room at Poole in Dorset, being the
property of Lodge of Amity No 137

show that Peter Vandyke was born in 1729 and came to England at the invitation of Sir Joshua Reynolds from whom, like Beach, he worked. He would have been in his early fifties at the time the portrait was painted. They also confirm that it was Peter who went to live in Bristol where he established a successful practice. Peter exhibited at the Incorporated Society of Artists and at the Free Society of Artists and some of his work is in the National Gallery. Also note the spelling of the surnames – Philip Van Dyke and Peter Vandyke.

Beach was born at Milton Abbass in Dorset and later settled at Bath and exhibited at the Royal Academy.

'Van Dyke' was initiated on 1 December 1777 in Caledonian Lodge No 134 which met at the Barbican Tavern, London Wall, and was exalted in Durnovarian Chapter at Dorchester in 1783. His Christian name in the Grand Lodge Membership Register is given as Philip!

Beach was initiated in Royal Cumberland Lodge on 6 October 1789 and the fees were waived 'in consideration of his very valuable present' to the lodge of the portrait of Dunckerley. He was raised on 20 October 1789.

Among other notable paintings by Beach were those of Mrs Sarah Siddons, the great tragedian actress, and George, Prince of Wales, a commission from whom was a tribute to his ability.

In 1808 the Hospitality Lodge No 248 (now the Royal Sussex Lodge of Hospitality No 187) paid four guineas for a portrait in oils of Dunckerley (*Fig* 22) and this hung in the Masonic Hall, Park Street, Bristol until November 1940 when the hall was completely gutted in an air raid and all the valuable and irreplaceable contents were destroyed.

Figure 22 (*Overleaf*)
This engraving of Dunckerley is from a Van Dyke painting which was at Freemasons' Hall, Park Street, Bristol. Unfortunately the hall and all its records were destroyed by enemy action in November 1940

Hofpitality Lodge
Nº 248 Jan.ry 27
AL 5812 AD 1808.

31

THE PUBLIC FACE

PUBLIC APPEARANCES and processions by lodge members were regarded as of recruiting value by Dunckerley and in his capacity as Provincial Grand Master he laid the foundation stones of several churches.

At Bristol on 17 August 1789 it was estimated that more than 50,000 people were present when he laid the cornerstone of St Paul's Church, Portland Square.

Freemasons from the City and other provinces assembled at the Merchant Taylors' Hall and were led by a band to the site of the new church. It was a time of industrial progress and development and the north-east corner-stone was raised by an 'engine for the purpose' and it was lowered on to a suitably inscribed plate and a variety of coins and medals.

According to a newspaper report 'The Provincial Grand Master gave three strokes with his Hiram upon which the Grand Chaplain implored a blessing upon such a joyous undertaking.' The report continues

> The P.G. Master then delivered over to the architect the various implements of architecture, with instructions and directions how to proceed in the work with which he is entrusted. After which the following lines were sung to the tune of *Rule Britannia*.
>
> > To Heaven's high Architect all praise,
> > All praise and gratitude be given,
> > Who deigned the human soul to raise,
> > By mystic secrets sprung from Heav'n,
> > Sound! Sound aloud! the Great Jehovah's praise,
> > To Him the dome, the temple raise.
>
> The innumerable spectators testified their approbation by loud and repeated joyful acclamations. This sacred and solemn ceremony

ended with a blessing from the Grand Chaplain. The Brethren then proceeded to St. James's Church, where the service was read by the Rev. D. Horndon, and a sermon from the XIIIth chap. of I Cor. 2 and 3 ver., was preached by the Grand Chaplain, the Rev. Brother Joseph Atwell Small, D.D., minister of the Church.

During the service a Masonic hymn and a hymn upon his Majesty's happy recovery (written by the P.G. Master) were sung by the choir.

The fraternity then returned to the Merchant Taylors' Hall where a sumptuous and elegant dinner was provided by Brother Weeks of the Bush Tavern. The greatest harmony and good humour and brotherly love prevailed, and the Brethren departed at an early hour not without uniting in the grand design of being happy themselves, and communicating happiness to others.

And the brethren communicated happiness to a masonic widow by sending her £21.

The inscription on the plate read:

The North-East Corner-Stone of the Chancel of this Church dedicated to the Service of God and called after his Apostle St. Paul. Was laid with all the Honors of Masonry, on Monday, the 17th. of August A.L. 5793 – A.D. 1789. A.R.G. III. 29 (Being the celebration of the Birth-Day of His Royal Highness Frederick Duke of York – A Free and accepted Mason). By Thomas Dunckerley Esq., P.G.M. for the City and County of Bristol, assisted by his Deputy Joshua Springer.
And John Hopkins
And Henry Jefferies *G.W.*

The architect, Daniel Hague, had been initiated two days before in the Lodge of Hospitality, when Dunckerley gave 'a most excellent charge'.

The following interesting account of the laying of the foundation stone of All Saints' Church, Southampton, appeared in the *Freemasons' Magazine* in 1794.

It was taken from the records of the Medina Lodge No 35.

On the 3rd. of August, 1792, in complyance with the request of Our Right Worshipful Provincial Grand Master Thomas Dunckerley, Esquire; made known by public Advertisement, the following Brethren now, and formerly belonging to this Lodge, in their proper

Provincial Cloathing and Jewels, attended by the Tyler, joined the Provincial Grand Lodge of Concord, opened by Our said Provincial Grand Master at Southampton, and preceded by a Band of Musick and a number of Operative Masons, went in procession to the Audit House, where being graciously received by Sir Yelverton Peyton, Mayor, the Aldermen and Corporation and Clergy of the Town and Neighbourhood, an Oration in praise of Masonry was delivered by Brother Jeans and a suitable Ode sung.

The Worshipful Mayor and Corporation, with all the Lodges assembled, then proceeded to Saint Hollyrood's Church where an excellent Sermon, applicable to the purpose of the meeting, was preached by Brother James Scot, and Sundry select pieces of sacred Musick, with the Coronation Anthem, performed by a Band of Fifty Vocal and Instrumental Performers; after which the Procession proceeded to the Scite of the Church of All Saints, in order to lay the Foundation Stone of the New Church, which was Masonickly done by Our Provincial Grand Master, in the presence of the Brethren, Mayor, Corporation, Clergy, and many thousand Spectators assembled on this occasion, who decently testified their joy thereat.

Sundry Coins and Medals in a Box, also an Inscription Plate, together with the History of the Town of South'ton. engrossed on Parchment and inclosed in a Christial Vial, being deposited under the Foundation Stone at the South West Corner. An Anthem purposely composed was then sung, as was Brittania Rule the Waves; Afterwards the Mayor and Corporation returned to the Audit House and the Brethren to the Grand Lodge, which was closed in due form.

The Medena Lodge being the oldest Lodge present, in conformity to a resolution of the Grand Lodge, took precedence of all other Lodges in the Procession of this day, the Lodge Concord excepted, in the Order following:

Wm. Bennet, Tyler, Apron lined with Garter Blue. John Major and Geo. M. Rose (Stewards) with white Wands & Aprons lined with crimson. Lancelot Foquet, Treasurer & Everhard Stock, Secretary. Robert Fabian, S. Warden & Isham Chapman, J. Warden. Wm. Holloway, Dy. Prov'l Grand Master P. Temp. All in White Gloves. Aprons lined with Garter Blue.

The Brethren to the number of One hundred and fifty, together with his Worship the Mayor and several of the Corporation, dined in perfect harmony at the Public Rooms, attended by a Band of Musick.

After dinner the Operative Masons to be employed in rebuilding the Church of All Saints, bearing their real working Tools, preceded by their Officers with their proper Attributes entered the Room and received a suitable Charge respecting the Work they had undertaken; and being refreshed and complimented, with great decorum, returned to their Habitations. The Brethren and Gentlemen assembled, finished the day in the most social manner and parted early in the Evening, having previously obtained permission of Brothers Jeans and Scot to print their Excellent Oration and Sermon delivered at the Audit House and Saint Holyrood's Church.

It was estimated that 10,000 people were at the ceremony.

Theatre performances with masonic allusions were popular and, like Provincial Grand Lodges, were announced in advance in the newspapers.

The *Bristol Gazette* of 29 June 1786 carried this advertisement.

THEATRE ROYAL, BRISTOL
At the particular request of Thomas Dunckerley Esq.
Prov. G.M. and by the particular desire of the City and
County, and of the several Lodges in this City of the most
ancient and honourable Society of Free and Accepted Masons.
For the Benefit of Brother Floor, Prompter;
On Friday next the 30th. June 1786 will be delivered a
Masonic Oration. By Brother Murray. To conclude with an
Ode, the Music composed by Mr. Boyton. The different Lodges
will be on the stage in their proper Cloathing, while the
Oration and the Ode are performing. After which will be
performed a Comedy called
The School for Wives.
(Names of performers were given)
To which will be added a Musical Entertainment of two Acts,
called
The Son in Law
To begin precisely at half-past Six o'clock.

The *Bristol Journal* of 18 August 1767 advertised a new satirical lecture on Hearts 'to which will be added a medical dissertation on Noses'. Included in the list of parts of the body to be dealt with was 'A Freemasons Heart'.

A new freemasons' epilogue concluded the entertainment.

32

THE CHARGES OF A MAN OF FAITH

A PICTURE OF Dunckerley as a man of strong faith with positive ideas as to the conduct expected of freemasons is gained from two of his orations which have survived.

The first was delivered on 28 April 1757 on the occasion of the opening of a new lodge room at Plymouth. It was then printed and advertised for sale in the *Gentleman's Magazine* as '*The Light and Truth of Freemasons Explained*. By T. Dunckerley. 6d. Published by Davey and Law.'

Only two copies are believed to remain. One was sold by auction in London in October 1945 and bought by the United Grand Lodge of England for 21 guineas. The cover of this is reproduced by permission of the Board of General Purposes (*Fig* 24), and the text reads as follows.

The Light and Truth of Masonry Explained

Light and Truth being the great essentials of the Royal Craft, I shall begin this discourse (prepared for the opening of this room) with that awful message which St. John delivered to the world, That God is Light, and in him no darkness at all; and that we are not worthy of the true fellowship, unless we walk in the Light, and do the Truth. O! sacred Light! whose orient beams make manifest that Truth which unites all good and faithful Masons in a heavenly Fellowship!

This sublime part of Masonry is that firm base on which is raised the shaft of Faith, that supports a beautiful entablature of good works: it is the foundation of a superstructure unbounded as the universe, and durable as eternity. To attempt a description of this stupendous fabrick may seem presumptuous in me, who have been so few years a Mason; but as you, my Brethren, were pleased to request something of this kind, give me leave to assure you that I am truly sensible of the honour; and though there are several among you, who by knowledge and long experience are well qualified for such an undertaking, yet as it is my duty to execute your commands, I shall cheerfully begin the work; and humbly hope by patience and industry to make some amends for the little time I have served.

The Light and Truth which St. John takes notice of in his message to the World, being a principal part of sublime Masonry, I have, as I observed before, taken it for the subject of my discourse, on this solemn occasion. I intreat you to hear me with attention; and whatever deficiencies you may discover in this Essay impute it to inexperience, and admonish me with Brother Love, that while I am pleasing the cause of Truth I may be free from error.

God said let there be Light; and there was Light. Without it the rude matter of Chaos, though brought into form, would still have been to little purpose. Let your Light so shine before men, that they may see your good works, was the advice of him that was a Light to lighten the Gentiles. Our Lights are not hid, but placed on Candlesticks; and these are silent monitors continually intimating to us, that as the ancient and honourable badge we wear has placed us above the rest of mankind, so all our duties to our Heavenly Master, our fellow creatures, and ourselves should be formed and contrived by the wisdom of God's word: strengthened and supported by Love, Truth and Charity; and beautified and adorned by Honesty, Temperance, and true Politeness. All Masons that are, or ever have been, were shewn the Light: and though they cannot forget it, yet alas! how faintly does it shine in the hearts of too many! How is its lustre sullied, and splendor diminished, by the folly, stupidity and madness of irreligion and impiety! These are the persons of whom St. John says they went out from us: but they were not of us: for if they had been of us, they would no doubt have continued with us; but they went out, that they might be made manifest that they were not all of us. And thus it is that those who depart from the Light bring an evil report on the Craft.

Truth, as it is a divine attribute, so is the foundation of all Masonic Virtues. It is one of our grand Principles; for to be good men and true, is part of the first great lesson we are taught: and at the commencement of our Freedom we are exhorted to be fervent and zealous in the pursuit of Truth and Goodness. It is not sufficient that we walk in the Light, unless we do the Truth also. All hypocrisy and deceit must be banished from among us: they are sincerity and

THE
LIGHT and TRUTH
OF
MASONRY
EXPLAINED,

In a CHARGE deliver'd to the Antient and
Honourable Society of

Free and *Accepted* MASONS,

AT

The POPE's-HEAD Tavern in *Plymouth*,
On the Dedicating and Opening

𝔄 new 𝔏odge=𝔕oom.

APRIL the 28th, 1757.

ALSO,

The MORAL PART of

MASONRY
EXPLAINED,
In a CHARGE

Deliver'd at the fame Lodge on the 24th of *June*, 1757;
being the Feaft of the Nativity of

St. *JOHN* the Baptift.

By *THOMAS DUNCKERLEY*,
Mafter of the LODGE.

The SECOND EDITION.

LONDON : Printed for P. DAVEY, and B. LAW, in
Ave-Mary-Lane, and fold by R. HAYDON in *Plymouth.*
MDCCLVIII. [*Price Six-pence.*]

Figure 23
The title page of *The Light & Truth of Masonry*

plain-dealing that complete the harmony of a Lodge, and render us acceptable in the sight of Him unto whom all hearts are open, all desires known, and from whom no secrets are hid. There is a charm in Truth that draws and attracts the mind continually toward it. The more we discover, the more we desire; and the great reward is Wisdom, Virtue, and Happiness. This is an edifice founded on a rock, which malice cannot shake or time destroy.

What a secret satisfaction is it to Masons, when in searching for Truth, they find the rudiments of all useful knowledge still preserved among us, as it has descended by oral tradition from the earliest ages: and to find likewise this Truth corroborated by the testimonies of the best and greatest men the world has produced. But this is not all; the Sacred Writings confirm what I assert, the sublime part of our Antient Mystery being there to be found; nor can any Christian Brother be a perfect Mason that does not make the word of God his study. Indeed we own all Masons as Brothers be they Christian, Jews or Mohametans (for Masonry is universal, and not strictly confined to any particular faith, sect or mode of worship): all Masons I say, of whatever religious denomination, who rule their passions and affections, and square their actions accordingly are acknowledged by us as Brothers, but, for our parts, the Holy Scripture is to be studied by us, and occasionally read and consulted.

Since without Light we cannot perceive the beauty and excellency of Truth and since we are certain that no man can be a worthy Brother who is wanting in either; it may not be improper at this Time to draw the character of him Who walks in Light and does the Truth; and who, according to St. John's Account, is worthy of the true fellowship.

As we call any building or piece of architecture perfect which hath all its parts, and is finished and completed according to the nicest rules of art; a Brother is in like manner said to be a good Mason who has studied and knows himself, and has learnt and practises that first and great lesson of subduing his Passions and Will, and tries to the utmost of his power to free himself from all vices, errors, and imperfections; not only those that proceed from the heart, but likewise all other defects of the understanding which are caused by custom, opinion, prejudice, or superstition; He who asserts the native freedom of his mind, and stands fast in the liberty that makes him free, whose soul is (if one may so express it), universal and well contracted, and who despises no man on account of his Country or Religion, but is ready at all times to convince the world that Truth,

Brotherly Love, and affording relief, are the grand principles on which he acts.

His whole life will be conformable and agreeable to that true light, and Law of God, which shines clear to his heart, and is the model by which he squares his judgement. In his outward behaviour he will be very careful not to give private or public offence, and (as far as appears to him right) will strictly comply with the laws, the customs, and religious institutions of the country in which he resides. To all mankind he will act upon the square; and do to others as he would have them do unto him. He will be firm and consistent with himself, and continually in expectation and on his guard against all accidents to which this life is exposed, and in particular he will by a well spent life be daily preparing for death, that final period of human action, which sooner or later will take us hence, to give a strict account of our stewardship and the improvement of our talents.

In fine, all good Masons should be pious, prudent, just and temperate, and resolutely virtuous.

From what I have advanced, and from these our ancient charges, I hope it is evident to everyone at the present, that it is the duty of every Mason to live soberly, righteously and godly; or, according to the words of the Evangelist, He should walk in the Light, and do the Truth. Continue, My Brethren, to persevere in principles that are disinterest, and I doubt not but you will find this room which we have now opened and dedicated to Masonry constantly resorted to by the wise, the faithful and the good.

Let us consider the intention of our meetings; let submission to your Officers and Brotherly Love to each other be shown by your diligent attendance in the Lodge and be very careful to enquire into the characters and capacities of those who are desirous to be admitted among you.

Study the Constitutions and Charges, and improve in the Fifth Science as far as your abilities and several avocations will permit. Have universal Benevolence and Charity for all mankind, and wherever you meet your necessitous Brethren disperse relieve them to the utmost of your ability, remembering, notwithstanding, not to do things that may really prejudice yourselves or families.

Let us by well-doing put to silence the ignorance of foolish men.

As free, but not using your liberty for a cloke of Maliciousness, but as the servants of God. Honour all Men, Love the Brotherhood, Fear God, Honour the King.

A charge delivered at Marlborough

Again taken from the *Freemasons' Magazine* is a charge on similar lines which Dunckerley delivered to 'the members of the Lodge of Free and Accepted Masons, at the Castle Inn, Marlborough, at a meeting for the distribution of charity to 24 poor people, at which most of the ladies in Marlborough were present'. It was on 11 September 1769.

Based on the text 'Blessed is he that considereth the poor' the charge read

It is with the greatest satisfaction I meet you here in the cause of charity; Charity is the basis of our Order; it is for this purpose we have a Grand Lodge at London, another at Edinburgh, and a third at Dublin. Lodges are now held on every part of this globe, and charities are collected and sent to the respective Grand Lodge of each Kingdom or state: there the distress'd brethren apply and find relief: nor is any exception made to difference of country or religion.

For, as in the sight of God we are all equally his children, having the same common parent and preserver – so we, in like manner, look on every Free-Mason as our brother; nor regard where he was born or educated, provided he is a good man, an honest man, which is 'the noblest work of God.'

A laudable custom prevailed among our ancient brethren; after they had sent their donations to the general charities, they considered the distresses of those in particular that resided in their respective neighbourhoods, and assisted them with such a sum as could be conveniently spared from the lodge. In humble imitation of this masonic principle, I recommend the present charity to your consideration; to which you readily and unanimously consented. The sum is, indeed, but small: yet when it is considered that this lodge is in its infant state; having been constituted but little more than three months: I hope, as the widow's mite was acceptable, this act of ours will be considered, not with respect to the sum, but the principles by which we are influenced.

I have told you in the lodge, and I repeat it now, that brotherly-love, relief and truth, are the grand principles of Masonry, and as the principal part of the company are unacquainted with the original intention of this society, it may be proper for their information, and your instruction, that I explain those principles, by which it is our duty in particular to be actuated.

By Brotherly-love, we are to understand that generous principle of the soul, which respects the human species as one family, created by an All-wise Being, and placed on this globe for the mutual assistance of each other. It is this attractive principle, or power that draws men together and united them in bodies politic, families, societies, and the various orders and denominations among men. But as most of these are partial, contracted or confined to a particular country, religion, or opinion; our Order, on the contrary, is calculated to unite mankind as one family: High and low, rich and poor, one with another; to adore the same God, and observe his law. All worthy members of this society are free to visit every lodge in the world; and though he knows not the language of the country, yet by a silent universal language of our own, he will gain admittance, and find that true friendship, which flows from the brotherly-love I am now describing.

At that peaceable and harmonious meeting he will hear no disputes concerning religion or politics; no swearing; no obscene, immoral or ludicrous discourse; no other contention but who can work best, who can agree best.

To subdue our passions, and improve in useful scientific knowledge; to instruct the younger brethren, and initiate the unenlightened, are principal duties in the lodge; which when done, and the word of God is closed, we indulge with the song and cheerful glass, still observing the same decency and regularity, with strict attention to the golden mean – believing with the poet that –

> 'God is paid when man receives,
> T' enjoy is to obey.'

Let me travel from east to west, or between north and south, when I meet a true brother I shall find a friend, who will do all in his power to serve me, without having the least view of self-interest: and if I am poor and in distress, he will relieve me to the utmost of his power, interest and capacity. This is the second grand principle; for, relief will follow where there is brother-love.

I have already mentioned our general charities as they are at present conducted, it remains now that I consider particular donations given from private lodges, either to those who are not masons or to a brother in distress. And first, with respect to a Charity like this before us, perhaps it is better to be distributed in small sums, that more may receive the benefit, than to give it in larger sums, which confine it to few.

With regard to a brother in distress, who should happen to apply to this lodge, or any particular member for relief, it is necessary that I inform you in what manner you are to receive him. And here I cannot help regretting, that such is the depravity of the human heart, there is no religion or society free from bad professors, or unworthy members, for as it is impossible for us to read the heart of man, the best regulated societies may be imposed on, by the insinuations of the artful and hypocrisy of the abandoned. It should therefore by no means lessen the dignity and excellency of the royal craft, because it is our misfortune to have bad men among us, any more than the purity and holiness of the Christian religion should be doubted, because too many of the wicked and profligate approach the holy altar.

Since, therefore, these things are so: be careful whenever a brother applies for relief, to examine strictly whether he is worthy of acceptance: enquire the cause of his misfortunes, and if you are satisfied they are not the result of vice or extravagance, relieve him with such a sum as the lodge shall think proper, and assist him with your interest and recommendation, that he may be employed according to his capacity, and not eat the bread of idleness.

This will be acting consistent with TRUTH, which is the third grand principle of Masonry.

TRUTH is a divine attribute, and the foundation of all masonic virtues: to be good men and true, is part of the first great lesson we are taught; and at the commencement of our freedom, we are exhorted to be fervent and zealous in the practice of truth and goodness. It is not sufficient that we walk in the light, unless we do the truth. All hypocrisy and deceit must be banished from us. Sincerity and plain dealing compleat the harmony of the brethren, within and without the lodge; and will render us acceptable in the sight of that great Being, unto whom all hearts are open, all desires known and from whom no secrets are hid.

There is a charm in truth that draws and attracts the mind continually towards it: the more we discover, the more we desire, and the great reward is, wisdom, virtue and happiness.

This is an edifice founded upon a rock, which malice cannot shake, or time destroy. What a secret satisfaction do we enjoy, when in searching for truth, we find the first principles of useful science, still preserved among us, as we received them, by oral tradition from the earliest ages; and we also find this truth corroborated by the testimonies of the best and greatest men the world has produced. But this is not all; the sacred writings confirm what I assert; the sublime part of our ancient mystery being there to be found nor can any Christian brother be a good Mason that does not make the word of God his first principal study.

I sincerely congratulate you on the happy establishment of this lodge, and the prospect you have of its utility and permanency, by the choice you have made of members capable to conduct it. Let Wisdom direct you to contrive for the best. Strengthen the cause of Masonry, by mutual Friendship, which is the companion and support of fraternal love, and which will never suffer any misunderstanding to inflame a brother, or cause him to behave unbecoming a member of our peaceable and harmonious society. Let us then resolve to beautify and adorn our Order, by discharging the duties of our respective stations, as good subjects, good parents, good husbands, good masters, and dutiful children; for by so doing we shall put to silence the reproaches of foolish men. As you know these things, brethren, happy are ye if ye do them; and thrice happy shall I esteem it to be looked on as the founder of a society in Marlborough whose grand principles are, brother-love, relief, and truth.

Let us consider these poor persons as our brothers and sisters, and be thankful to Almighty God, that he has been pleased to make us his instruments of affording them this small relief; most humbly supplicating the Grand Architect of the UNIVERSE, from whom all holy desires, all good counsels and all just works do proceed, to bless our undertaking, and grant that we may continue to add some little comfort to the poor of this town.

Next to the Deity, whom can I so properly address myself to as the most beautiful part of the creation?

You have heard, Ladies, our grand principles explained, with the instructions given to the brethren; and I doubt not but at other times you have heard many disrespectful things said of this society. Envy, malice, and all uncharitableness will never be at a loss to decry, find fault, and raise objections to what they do not know. How great then are the obligations you lay on this lodge! With what superior esteem, respect, and regard, are we to look on every lady present, that has done us the honour of her company this evening. To have the sanction of the fair is our highest ambition, as our greatest care will be to preserve it. The virtues of humanity are peculiar to your sex;

and we flatter ourselves the most splendid ball could not afford you greater pleasure, than to see the human heart made happy, and the poor and distrest obtain present relief.

33

THE SPIRIT OF THE FESTIVE BOARDS

THERE WAS ALSO a free and easy side to Dunckerley who was a man of amiable nature. He enjoyed the social aspect of freemasonry and believed that brethren got to know the true character of each other when they met informally outside the lodge.

The festive boards were enlivened by music and song perhaps even more than today, and Provincial Grand Master Dunckerley although cognisant of dignity his office was by no means sombre. Life at sea when the ship's crew sang as they worked and had to provide their own entertainment made him a good mixer and he was blessed with a fine voice and frequently entertained the brethren with song. More than one account of Provincial Grand Lodges report that at the dinner which followed mirth, good humour and jollity prevailed and that 'a number of excellent good songs were sung by Brother Dunckerley'.

The dinners were well supported. At Dorset in June 1780 56 tickets were sold at 5s and £1 1s went to the 'paid singers' and 'paid musick' cost £2 12s 6d which indicates the presence of a small band or ensemble.

The honouring of toasts were often accompanied by a song or the reciting of a verse, one being

Charge, brethren! Charge your glasses to the top,
My toast forbids the spilling of a drop,
'Tis to that fair, illustrious Blaze of Light,
Whose Royal Beams dispel the shade of night.

And there was a separate toast for every officer there ever was. Royal birthdays were accepted as occasions to assemble the brethren and Dunckerley was in Bristol on 16 August 1792 when he called the Masons of the province to the Bush Tavern to do honour to the Duke of York. The festive board toast list was.

The King and the Craft
The Queen
His Royal Highness, the Prince of Wales, Grand Master
His Royal Highness, the Duke of York, with a thrice hearty wish that he may experience many happy returns of this day, and that when dire necessity calls he may lead the army of Great Britain to the conquest of her enemies
The Duke of Clarence, and the wooden walls of Old England
Prince Edward, the Grand Patron of Knight Templars
Lord Rawdon, Acting Grand Master of England
Mrs. Dunckerley, Lady Patroness of Masonry in this City etc.

The reference to Grand Master and Acting Grand Master may seem a little confusing. Lord Rawdon, who afterwards became Earl of Moira and later Marquess of Hastings, served under the Prince. His Royal Highness once referred to him as the friend he admired and hoped he might long live to superintend the government of the Craft and extend its principles.

The toast list for gathering of Knights Templar and Royal Arch Masons read

The King and the Craft
The Prince of Wales Grand Master of Symbolic Masonry
His Royal Highness the Duke of York, with a thrice hearty wish that His Royal Highness may be blest with health and happiness, and long remain a terror to the enemies of Great Britain.
The Duke of Clarence, Grand Patron of Royal Arch Masons
Prince Edward, Grand Patron of Knight Templars

The Queen, Princesses, the Duchess of York and all the Royal Family.

Earl of Moira and Sir Peter Parker.

Lord Howe and the Wooden walls of Old England.

(Admiral Sir Peter Parker was the Deputy Grand Master for 25 years from 1786.)

Initiates in the eighteenth century were welcomed into freemasonry with the singing of The Enter'd 'Prentices Song. It was written by Bro Matthew Birkhead who died sometime before December 1722 when the song was published in *Read's Weekly Journal*.

It was reproduced in *Anderson's Constitutions* the following year with six verses but a little later another verse was added.

When it was printed in the *Freemasons Pocket Companion* of 1738 there was the instruction that it was 'To be fung when all grave bufinefs is over, and with the Mafter's Leave'.

It is certain that Dunckerley, with his love for verse and song, would have encouraged the singing of the Entered Apprentice Song, and it is a pleasing thought that, written over 260 years ago, it is still sung by the brethren of some of our older lodges to greet newly-made Masons on the most important night of their masonic career.

After the singing of the penultimate verse the brethren rise and join hands and after the last verse re-sing the last two lines of each verse.

Over the years there have been a few variations in some of the wording, but the words which follow are the original as composed by Brother Birkhead.

Come let us prepare,
We brothers that are
Assembled on merry occasion:
Let's drink, laugh, and sing;
Our wine has a spring:
Here's a health to an Accepted Mason.

The world is in pain
Our secrets to gain;
But still let them wonder and gaze on:
They ne'er can divine
The word or the sign
Of a Free and an Accepted Mason.

'This this and 'tis that,
They cannot tell what,
Why so many great men in the nation
Should aprons put on
To make themselves one
With a Free and an Accepted Mason.

Great kings, dukes and lords,
Have laid by their swords,
Our mystery to put a good grace on;
And ne'er been asham'd
To hear themselves nam'd
With a Free and an Accepted Mason.

Antiquity's pride
We have on our side,
Which maketh men just in their station:
There's nought but what's good
To be understood
By a Free and an Accepted Mason.

We're true and sincere,
And just to the fair,
Who will trust us on ev'r occasion.
No mortal can more
The ladies adore,
Than a Free and an Accepted Mason.

Then join hand in hand,
To each other firm stand;
Let's be merry and put a bright face on:
What mortal can boast, So noble a toast,
As a Free and an Accepted Mason?

By permission of Provincial Grand Master Dunckerley the following was rendered by Brother Asperne at a Grand Lodge for Essex in 1793. The tune was 'Derry Down'.

All you who love order, attend to my song,
And if you'll be patient, I'll not keep you long,
'Tis of Heads and of Bodies I now mean to sing;
For a Head without Body's a very strange thing.
        Derry down, &c.

In the Lodge when we Brothers in Masonry meet,
To hear the grave lecture with good sense replete,
If the Master cries "Order!" no more's to be said,
Which proves very clearly that he is the Head.
        Derry down, &c.

May the Head and the Body unanimous be;
For the Head and the Body should ne'er disagree;
The Head, of the Body, should ne'er be in dread,
'Tis a very bad Body would cut off a Head.
        Derry down, &c.

May Britain respect then the Head and the Laws,
And may Englishmen ever be firm in their cause;
May her sons ride triumphantly Head o'er the waves,
And that Body chastise that would make them its slaves.
        Derry down, &c.

And thus having come to the end of my Song,
As a Body of men let us never do wrong;
But, to keep all our enemies ever in dread,
Make the Subjects of Body, the Sov'reign the Head.
        Derry down, &c.

Figure 24
A song written for 1793 Provincial Grand Lodge of Essex

34

CONSTITUTING LODGES

WHEN DUNCKERLEY FIRST became a Provincial Grand Master there were about 245 lodges throughout the country, but each year the number increased.

Then, as now, there was a set form for constituting new lodges and the following is taken from a pocket companion which was published in 1738. Modern spelling is substituted for the old.

A new lodge, for avoiding many irregularities, should be solemnly constituted by the Grand Master, with his Deputy and Wardens; or in the Grand Master's absence, the Deputy shall act for his Worship, and shall choose some Master of a lodge to assist him; or in case the Deputy is absent, the Grand Master shall call forth some Master of a lodge to act as Deputy pro tempore.

The candidates, or the new Master, and Wardens, being yet among the Fellow Craft, the Grand Master shall ask his Deputy if he has examined them, and finds the candidate master well skill'd in the Noble Science and the Royal Art, and duly instructed in our mysteries, etc.

And the Deputy answering in the affirmative, he shall (by the Grand Master's order) take the candidate from among his Fellows, and present him to the Grand Master, saying, Right Worshipful Grand Master, the Brethren here desire to be formed into a new lodge; and I present this my worthy brother to be their Master; whom I know to be of good morals and great skill, true and trusty, and lover of the whole fraternity, wheresoever dispersed over the face of the earth.

Then the Grand Master, placing the candidate on his left hand, having asked and obtained the unanimous consent of all the brethren, shall say, 'I constitute and form these good brethren into a new lodge, and appoint you the Master of it, not doubting your capacity

151

and care to preserve the cement of the lodges,' etc., with some other expressions that are proper and usual on that occasion, but not proper to be written.

Upon this the Deputy shall rehearse the charges of a Master, and the Grand Master shall ask the candidate; saying, 'Do you submit to these charges, as Masters have done in all ages?' and the candidate signifying his cordial submission there-unto, the Grand Master shall, by certain significant ceremonies and antient usages, install him, and present him with the constitutions, the lodge book, and the instruments of his office, not all together, but one after another; and after each of them, the Grand Master, or his Deputy, shall rehearse the short and pithy charge that is suitable to the thing presented.

After this the members, of this new lodge, bowing all together to the Grand Master, shall return his Worship thanks, and immediately do their homage to their new Master, and signify their promise of subjection and obedience to him by the usual congratulation.

The Deputy and the Grand Wardens, and any other brethren present, that are not members of this new lodge, shall next congratulate the new Master; and he shall return his becoming acknowledgements to the Grand Master first, and to the rest in their order.

Then the Grand Master desires the new Master to enter immediately upon the exercise of his office, in choosing his wardens: and the new Master, calling forth two fellow craft, presents them to the Grand Master for his approbation, and to the new lodge for their consent. And that being granted,

The senior or junior Grand Wardens, or some Brother for him, shall rehearse the charges of wardens; and the candidates, being solemnly asked by the new Master, shall signify their submission thereunto.

Upon which the new Master, presenting them with the instruments of their office, shall, in due form, install them in their proper places; and the brethren of that new lodge shall signify their obedience to the new wardens by the usual congratulation.

And this lodge, being thus completely constituted, shall be registered and the Grand Master's Book, and by his order notified to the other lodges."

That is the basis on which the present ceremony of constituting a lodge has been formulated.

Repulsing cowans and intruders

As now, lodges had to be on the alert for cowans and intruders. On 22 November 1768 Grand Lodge were warned that many idle persons were travelling the country, some dressed as Turks or Moors and under the sanction of certificates 'and pretending to be distressed Masons imposed upon the benevolence of many lodges and brethren'.

Incidents in his provinces were reported by Dunckerley and he requested Grand Lodge to issue this warning in their quarterly communication.

> That a person travelling by the name of Clark, who some time since kept a tavern in London having fraudently obtained money from the lodge at Wells; Notice of the same is given to prevent further imposition: and whereas several persons disguised like Turks who pretend they were made prisoners in attempting to relieve Gibraltar, have imposed on Lodges at Bristol and Bath; notice of the same is hereby given that such itinerant mendicants may be detected.

35

THE FAMILY MAN

THERE ARE FEW details of Dunckerley's private life but those which are available indicate a happy marriage and that he was a thoughtful husband and father and concerned about provision for his family.

Before he made his quick flee to the Continent in HMS *Guadaloupe* he drafted the greater part of his naval pension to his wife.

Even in his last will and testament, made some 20 months before he died, thought for his family came before his personal wishes. His request was to be 'decently buried in the Temple Church near the Knights Templars' if he died within 20 miles of

London, but there was the proviso that if at a farther distance from London 'then it is my desire to be buried at the place or in that Parish or Churchyard where I may happen to depart this life as the carriage of my corpse to London might be attended with too great an expence'.

It is perhaps not surprising that, coming from a broken home and having been denied the fond attentions of a caring father, he married when only 20 years of age and then to a lady who was his senior by ten years.

He died in the year of their Golden Wedding. Mrs Dunckerley outlived him by five and a half years, dying aged 86 or 87 at Hampton Court Palace in February 1801.

Other than referring to 'my wife and children' Dunckerley makes no mention in letters which are still in existence to the number of children in his family. On a few occasions he speaks of a daughter, and a son is mentioned in a letter sent to him and reference to the son is also made in a few lodge minutes.

In a brief 'autobiography' which appeared in the *Freemasons' Magazine* in October 1793 reference is made to the expense of an operation undergone by his daughter adding to his financial stress in 1764. Owing to a fall she had to have her right leg amputated above the knee.

The assumption seems to have been there was only one daughter. Powell and Littleton in their *Freemasonry in Bristol* said the daughter married a Mr Ashfield Hunt who lived at 56 Park Street, Bristol, but do not say when and give no source for the information.

In a letter written from Salisbury on 19 January 1783 to his friend James Heseltine, the Grand Secretary, Dunckerley said.

> Mrs. D-------, my daughter and her husband unite with me in sincere wishes for ye health and happiness of yourself, Sister Heseltine and little folks . . .

Only two months later he commenced a second letter to Heseltine with these words.

> Mrs. Dunckerley and Mr. Edgar desire to unite with me in sincere

thanks for your kind concern and condolences on our much lamented loss. At the request of my son–in–law I have promised to remain with him, and in all probability shall pass the remainder of my days in this county; except a little time in each summer at Hampton Court.

The wording suggests the condolences were on the death of a daughter. If so were there two, one married to Mr Hunt and the other to Mr Edgar?

It is recorded in the Lord Steward's Papers for the period that Dunckerley's mother Mary recieved a Christmas bounty of £20 each year from 1735 to 1757. The Lord Steward's Papers are not complete and there may have been earlier payments of which no record has survived. It certainly seems there were payments after 1757 up to the time of her death in 1760, and Dunckerley wasted no time in his attempt to have the bounty transferred to her grand daughter who, of course, was his daughter.

Immediately after the funeral of his mother he contacted Sir Edward Walpole, the second son of Lady Walpole at whose house Mary had lived before her marriage. The next day Sir Edward gave Dunckerley the following introductory note which is still preserved in Grand Lodge Library. Unfortunately the addressee is not named.

Mr. Dunckerley who waits on you with this will easily be remembered by you, as he was made a gunner by you at my request. His mother had £10 a year on the Treasury Bounty List. She died t'other day. His daughter is a very unfortunate young creature through a melancholly accident which occasion'd her leg to be cut off and has flung her into a feeble state and rendered her incapable of afsisting herself.

While the vacancy on the list is yet unknown it would be a great charity to let the young woman whose names are the same Mary Dunckerley pafs on upon the list in the place of her grandmother. And I should hope not a very difficult matter.

I am your most obedient humble
serv^t Ed Walpole.

Pall Mall Jan 13 1760

The note refers to a bounty of £10 in January 1760 while the records to 1757 mention £20. The difference could be accounted for by a government economy drive which occurred as frequently in those days as they do now!

The method suggested for the transfer of this bounty to the granddaughter was, perhaps, not illegal but was certainly not strictly orthodox.

Sadly, however, there is nothing in the records to indicate whether the child ever received the Christmas bounty.

When the original Somerset House which had been used to accommodate people associated with the Court was replaced by a new building which was for government use only, pensions were introduced for those formerly provided with apartments, and warrant T6H/291 dated 9 October 1776 granted a pension of £45 a year to Miss Mary Ann Dunckerley.

Perhaps Dunckerley took advantage of a set of circumstances – eviction from their Somerset House apartment and ill–health – to obtain the pension for his daughter.

In a letter to the Grand Secretary on 9 January 1790 Dunckerley wrote that 'Mrs. Dunckerley and her grand daughter unite with me in wishing that Mrs. West and yourself may enjoy many happy returns of the season'.

The reference to 'her' and not 'our' granddaughter may appear rather strange but could be his manner of phraseology. On the other hand his wife could have been a widow when they were married some 45 years before with a son or daughter who had presented her with a grandchild.

There are also few references to Dunckerley's son and no evidence that there was more than one. The earliest mention is the Muster List of HMS *Vanguard* where it is shown that his son went to sea with him.

In 1767 Colonel Sir James Adolphus Oughton wrote in a letter to Dunckerley:'Lord Granby may get you a commission for your son, and will, I dare say (recommended as you are) do it readily; they advise you well not to ask a favour of him yourself'. At the time the Marquess of Granby was the Commander-in-Chief of the British Army.

Dunckerley made his approach to the top but searches of

military records have failed to reveal whether the son did receive a commission.

Three years before, in 1764, when Thomas fled to the Mediterranean in HMS *Gaudaloupe* the ship was joined at Guernsey on the outward voyage by a 17-year-old seaman by the name of Thomas Dunckerley. Another of the same name joined the ship at Mahon on 28 January 1765 leaving her at Cadiz on 13 April.

There is nothing to connect these two with our Dunckerley, but the 17-year-old was the right age to have been his son for he had then been married about 20 years. The youth left the ship at Leghorn at the north of the west coast of Italy on 11 January 1766. Our Dunckerley had been put ashore six months before because of illness.

It is not possible to check masonic records in Guernsey to ascertain if assistance was given to the boy for the oldest lodge, Mariners No 168, was not warranted until 1784.

In an article in the *Freemason's Quarterly Review* of 1842, it is stated

> Brother Dunckerley's Masonic example was lost on his son, whose follies embittered the last years of his existence. Extravagance straitened the means, disorderly conduct afflicted the mind of the fond, unhappy parent. Every means were tried, ineffectually, to reclaim the wretched son. At his father's death, there being no provision left, he became a wanderer and an outcast. Being a Mason, he was ever besieging lodges and individuals. At last he became a bricklayer's labourer, and was seen carrying a hod on his shoulder, ascending a ladder! This poor fellow's misfortunes and misconduct at length terminated, and the grandson of a king died in a cellar in St. Giles.

The story is supported to some extent by the occasional lodge minute. A Salisbury Lodge account book had this entry:

1779. Oct. 6. To Brother Dunckerley's son in distress 10s 6d.

The relief came from the Sarum Lodge.

From his wife Ann, Dunckerley received support in all his masonic activities. She accompanied him on several of his journeys and was appointed patroness of the Craft in a number of provinces and of the Knights Templar and during his illness she helped with the administration.

In several letters Dunckerley added that 'Mrs. D--- sends good wishes to her sister and brothers', the relationship being obviously masonic.

Ann Dunckerley's maiden name is not known. It is quite possible she was a native of Plymouth, where they lived for some years, and met Dunckerley when his ship was in port.

Unfortunately Plymouth was a wartime target and hundreds of buildings and irreplaceable documents were lost during the Second World War making research difficult or impossible.

36

PROUD TO CALL HIM BROTHER

AN ARTICLE WHICH appeared in the *Freemasons' Magazine* in October 1793, two years before the death of Dunckerley, gives reliable information. It was written by Brother Thomas White, a Master at Colchester University, who was described as 'a valued contributor'.

White was a member of the Angel Lodge which still meets at Colchester as No 51. At the Provincial Grand Lodge of Essex held on 12 August 1793 Provincial Grand Master Dunckerley demonstrated his confidence in White by investing him as the Junior Warden after he had served as the Provincial Grand Secretary for the previous year. Without doubt the information in the article was obtained from Dunckerley.

The heading on the article, 'Sketch of the Life of Thomas Dunckerley, Esq., P.G.M.' was followed by the quotation of

Right and Wrong he taught

Truths as refin'd as ever Athens heard;
And (strange to tell!) he practis'd what he preach'd
                                        – Armstrong

The article read

Mr. Dunckerley is a Past Senior Grand Warden of England, Provin-
cial Grand Master for the city and county of Bristol, the counties of
Dorset, Essex, Gloucester, Hereford, Somerset, Southampton, and
the Isle of Wight, under the authority of His Royal Highness the
Prince of Wales; Grand Superintendent and Past Grand Master of
Royal Arch Masons for the city and county of Bristol, the counties of
Dorset, Essex, Gloucester, Hereford, Kent, Nottingham, Somerset,
Southampton, Surrey, Suffolk, Sussex, and Warwick, under the
patronage of His Royal Highness the Duke of Clarence; Most
Eminent and Supreme Grand Master of Knights of Rosa Crucis,
Templars, Kadosh, &c., of England, under His Royal Highness
Prince Edward, Patron of the Order.

The Masonic titles of this gentleman are given to shew the high
sense the Grand Lodge of England entertains of his abilities and
exertions, the great trust reposed in him by the Heir Apparent and
his illustrious brothers, the very great esteem and regard with which
he is honoured (we had almost said adored) by several hundred
Brethren in the above-mentioned counties, and to point out the
amazing progress he has made in moral, social and scientific
Masonry, during forty-six years, by his travels in Europe, Africa, and
America, particularly in England, Ireland, France, Spain, Portugal,
Italy, Gibraltar, Corsica and Sardinia.

As a gentleman, Mr Dunckerley is universally allowed to possess
powerful mental abilities, which he has not failed to cultivate by an
intimate knowledge of the Belles Lettres, and those arts and sciences
that refine and exalt the human mind; and by a most extensive
intercourse and acquaintance with the most illustrious and ingenious
personages in this and many other kingdoms.

With a most enlightened mind and an urbanity of manners, that
endears him to everyone, he fulfils all the relative duties in a manner
truly exemplary. He has naturally a taste for poetry, and exclusive of
those pieces which have received the stamp of public approbation,
his private friends have infinite cause to be charmed with the effu-

sions of his Muse.

Though conversant in science and philosophical researches, he is of too virtuous and vigorous a frame of mind, and too well-grounded in his religious and moral principles ever to suffer philosophy to lead to infidelity; but all the Christian Truths receive his most hearty concurrence, and all the Christian Virtues his constant practice. As a Brother, Mr Dunckerley stands unrivalled in his indefatigable exertions in the glorious cause of Charity, and in promoting concord and unanimity, brotherly love, morality, and good fellowship, with the strictest order and decorum; witness his many private and public charities, particularly his recent donation at the Provincial Grand Lodge at Chelmsford, for the support of the Royal Cumberland Freemasons' School; witness also the many excellent charges he has given in the Provincial Grand Lodges where he has presided, and the uniform proofs his whole life has manifested, that he 'lets his light shine before men.'

The various scenes this gentleman has experienced would require volumes to record; the limits of our work will only admit of the general outlines of a character chequered with events, which could be sustained only by honesty and courage. 'Honestas et Fortitudo' was a motto he took at ten years of age, when a thirst for glory, and a desire to engage in the bustle of the world induced him to leave school abruptly and enter the Royal Navy, where, during twenty-six years constant service, he had the honour and satisfaction to obtain the commendations and friendship of the following gallant commanders under whom he served, viz., Admirals Sir John Norris, Matthews, and Martin, Captains Cornish, Russell, Berkley, Coates, Jekyll, Legge, Marshall, Byron, Swanton, Peyton, and Marlow, but having no parliamentary interest, nor any friend in power, that he then knew of, to assist him, his own modest merit was insufficient to procure him a command.

In the year 1760, upon Mr. Dunckerley's return from the siege of Quebec, an event happened which could not but fill him with astonishment; as it placed him in a new and most extraordinary point view. A Lady, receiving the Sacrament on her deathbed, made a declaration in all the awful solemnity of the occasion, by which it appeared that Mr. Dunckerley owed his birth to the first personage in the Kingdom, and Nature was determined that it never should be questioned, for those who recollect the high Personage alluded to, will require no further proof when they see the subject of these Memoirs; but as this is a matter of much delicacy, our readers must excuse us from entering into further particulars and permit us to draw a veil over this part of the life we propose to record, which were we at liberty to illustrate, would prove a most interesting part of the history.

Notwithstanding this discovery of Mr. Dunckerley's descent, he determined not to quit the service of his country until the end of the war, but, unfortunately for him, in the meantime the sudden dissolution of the great Personage we have alluded to, deprived him of a friend, who died without knowing that such a person existed. In 1764 he applied for and obtained superannuation; but it was not until 1767 that his case was laid before a Great Personage, who was graciously pleased to make a provision for him.

Possessing a strong active mind, with an easy fluent delivery, he was advised in the year, 1770, to become a student in the law, and during five years' close application, acquired such a fund of legal knowledge, that in Michaelmas term, 1774, he was called to the bar by the Honourable Society of the Inner Temple, but being fond of an active life, and still animated by a thirst for glory, when the court of France became hostile to this country in supporting American Independence, and an invasion was threatened, he accepted a commission in the South Hampshire regiment of Militia, where he greatly distinguished himself during three years service. It has been the particular good fortune of Mr. Dunckerley to be honoured with the friendship of the first and best characters of the age, from whom he has letters that would fill an octavo volume, and which reflect the highest honour upon him and them. We were anxious to obtain many of these to enrich our present work, but such is his extreme delicacy and fear of giving offence, that we could only obtain the two here subjoined; one if from a noble Viscount (now a Marquis) and the other from the late General Sir Adolphus Oughton, K.B., which we are happy in being permitted to publish, as they offer a just, tribute of praise to the benevolence of our gracious and beloved Sovereign, and manifest an interest and regard for Mr. Dunckerley, worthy of their exalted rank. Gratitude is a prominent feature in this gentleman's character, – We have felt the luxury of doing good when we have heard him speak of the many obligations he is under to the following noblemen and gentlemen, which he relates with a heart over-flowing with a just sense of their kindness and favours. In 1766 he was befriended by Lord William Gordon, Captain Charles Meadows (now Mr. Pierpoint), and Captain Edward Meadows, of the Royal Navy. In 1767 by the Dukes of Beaufort and Buccleugh,

Lord Chesterfield, Lord Harcourt, Lord Valentia, Sir Edward Walpole, Sir Edward Hawke, and Mr. Worsley. In 1768 by the Duke of Grafton, the Marquis of Granby, and Lord Townshend, and afterwards by Lord Bruce (now Earl of Aylesbury), Lord North, Mr. Robinson, Mr. Brummell, Mr. Richard Burke, Mr. Blackburn a merchant in the city, and Mr. Heseltine, our worthy Grand Treasurer; and though 'last not least' by General Hotham and Colonel Hulse, to whom he expresses himself highly obliged by their kindness and personal attention.

He married early in life, being now in the sixty-ninth year of his age, nearly forty-nine of which have been spent in wedlock; his lady, who is every way worthy of such a valuable husband, is some few years older than he is, and enjoys a good share of health and spirits. Having last year, in his Masonic character, laid the first stone of a new church at Southampton, he jocularly observed, 'that if the structure were completed by the time he had completed fifty years in wedlock, he should think himself justified in following the practice of some nations he had travelled in, viz., of keeping a Jubilee year, and in that case handsel the new church by being re-married in it.'

Previous to the appropriation of Somerset House to its present use, Mr. Dunckerley had apartments therein, since then he generally resides at his apartments in Hampton Court Palace, and by the munificence of his Sovereign, the Prince of Wales, and Duke of York, has the honour and happiness to be in a very comfortable situation, and, to crown all, we shall add in his own words, 'that he has been blessed with the friendship of that Great Being who never faileth those that seek Him.'

That he may long, very long, continue to enjoy these blessings, and be an ornament to a Society which has received the testimony of approbation for the good and great in all ages, is the free, fervent, and zealous wish of his humble Biographer, and thousands of others, who deem it none of the least of the prerogatives of Freemasonry to call this excellent man by the most friendly of all titles – A BROTHER.

37

EULOGISED AND DERIDED

ALL GREAT MEN have their faithful followers but also their critics
and for 200 years Dunckerley had been admired and praised
decried and criticised and some of these opinions should be
quoted as we examine the enigma of this great and immortal
freemason.

An article on him in the *Freemasons' Quarterly Review* of
1842 reads

> To the character of the well-bred gentleman, possessed of power-
> ful mental abilities, he united a knowledge of the belles-lettres, an
> acquaintance with scientific and philosophical researches, and that
> well-grounded comprehension of religion and moral principle which
> is the surest protection against infidelity. He was generous and
> hospitable to a fault, and the poor and needy Brother never applied
> to him vain.

The Somerset historian, the late W Bro W. G. Fisher, a member
of the Quatuor Coronati Lodge was not an admirer of Dunckerley. Of him he wrote in 1962: 'He was a vain man and seemed to
suffer from a mild illusion of grandeur.'

Brother Fisher made this concession, however: 'One thing is
certain, he introduced a new outlook in Provincial administration and although he persistently demanded support and loyalty
for Grand Lodge he also did what he could to see that the
Brethren giving that support and loyalty were rewarded. He was
greatly respected in the Province . . .'

Three years later came words which were not a credit to one
who was rightly honoured for his other masonic research.

How much longer are we going to perpetuate without examination, the story that he (Dunckerley) was the natural son of King George II? I began to look into the matter some time ago, but had to put it on one side owing to pressure of work. I soon discovered that the claim was made by Dunckerley himself, but not until after the death of his mother and of George II.

Brother Fisher should have been aware that Dunckerley did not know of his true parentage until after the death of his unfortunate and unselfish mother. King George II died soon after she did and while Thomas was at sea. Mrs Pinkney, who conveyed the information to Thomas, died just 15 months after Mary.

The three people who could substantiate the authenticity of his claim had departed this life all within the space of 15 months.

W Bro Lieut.-Colonel Eric Ward, of Quatour Coronati Lodge, who was the Prestonian Lecturer in 1970, has said of Dunckerley

> In some respect he was the greatest Mason we have had . . . Dunckerley could be described as the fore-runner of a distinguished line of dedicated mendicants, his successful appeals for subscriptions to one thing and another indicating that he must have possessed remarkable persuasive powers.
>
> It was out of this and due to Dunckerley that our present system of Provincial Grand Lodge officering came into being. The story is one which curiously seems to have been neglected, but it shows from the part Dunckerley played what a great psychologist he was also.

For his Prestonian Lecture in 1965 W Bro Edward Newton, the then Assistant Librarian to the United Grand Lodge of England, rightly included Thomas Dunckerley among the four 'Brethren who made Masonic History', stating that his constructive work did much towards bringing peace and resolution to the institution during a critical period.

Another Prestonian Lecturer, W Bro A. R. Hewitt (1967), who was also Librarian and Curator of the United Grand Lodge, felt that Dunckerley's services to Royal Arch Masonry were at least equal to those rendered to the Craft.

Brother Henry Sadler's estimation of Dunckerley comes

nearer the truth than that of any historian who has succeeded. In 1891 Sadler wrote

> Every branch of Masonry, as well as each province and lodge with which he identified himself, seems to have had an upward tendency from the moment of his taking an active part in its affairs. It will have been observed that prior to Dunckerley's coming to the front, the Grand Lodge itself had neither habitation, furniture, jewels, register, or a regular system of communication with the Provincial Lodges; and within a few years of his advent these wants and omissions were supplied.
>
> Although I have no desire to claim for him exclusive credit for these and many other improvements, I am fully satisfied that if they were not actually the outcome of his suggestions, by his earnest enthusiasm, methodical habits, energy and example, he did far more than anyone else towards bringing them about and establishing them as essentials in the Masonic system.

Robert Freke Gould, whose voluminous contribution to freemasonry must be admired can be placed among the non-admirers. Of Dunckerley's oration *The Light and Truth of Freemasonry Explained* he scathingly comments: 'Even if we concede that the lecture . . . was given . . . it proved very little, merely that Dunckerley was capable of stringing together a quantity of platitudes and constructing a sort of Masonic oration rather below than above the ordinary level of such performances.'

Gould goes on to refer to the opinions of Dunckerley expressed by the Rev Doctor George Oliver, the eminent nineteenth-century masonic archaeologist. Gould pays his only tribute to Dunckerley when he says 'he was a very worthy member of the Craft' but qualified this by saying, '. . . the loose statements of Dr. Oliver that "he (Dunckerley) was the oracle of the Grand Lodge and the accredited interpreter of its Constitutions"; also that "his decision was final on all points, both of doctrine and discipline" are simply untrue . . .'

I feel Gould does himself no credit when he infers that the rank of Past Grand Warden was conferred on Dunckerley 'out of respect to the Duke of Cumberland, Grand Master, whose uncle he was generally supposed to be'.

Another great masonic personality of the period, William Preston, wrote in his *Illustrations of Masonry*: 'By the indefatigable assiduity of that Masonic luminary, Thomas Dunckerley, Esq., in whose favour the appointment for Hampshire was first made, Masonry has made considerable progress, not only within his province but in many other counties in England.'

William Preston was the founder of the Prestonian Lectures. It is a pity one cannot be devoted solely to Thomas Dunckerley.

W Bro C. D. Rotch, in a paper on Dunckerley and the Lodge of Friendship, presented to the Quatuor Coronati Lodge in 1943, said Dunckerley's

> zeal and enthusiasm in his life work never flagged. . . . The establishment of the Lodge of Friendship and the Somerset House Lodge alone was an achievement of outstanding importance; if his provincial work is also considered, then surely Thomas Dunckerley must be regarded as the greatest Masonic builder of current times, perhaps of all time.

He saw Dunckerley as one who 'set out to make Masonry accessible to and appreciated by men of higher social position than had previously been possible and to secure their services for the direction and governing of Grand Lodge'.

Brother Albert F. Calvert in his account of 200 years of English Freemasonry, *The Grand Lodge of England 1717–1917*, does not give a great deal of space to Dunckerley, but even so he had this to say of him.

> His energy, example and genius for organisation rescued the office from the state of neglect and inutility into which it had fallen, and justly entitle him to be styled the father of the present race of Provincial Grand Masters.
>
> In addition to introducing the practice of holding lodges on board men o' war, to reviving the dignity and extending the utility of the Provincial Grand Mastership, to his yeoman service in helping to provide Grand Lodge with a habitation, a Register, furniture and jewels, Dunckerley had still further claims to be regarded as the most notable Masonic figure of the last half of the 18th. century. . . .

His great honesty, courage and singleness of purpose were of inestimable value to the Craft, his urbanity of manner and gift of friendship gained for him the confidence and esteem of a large circle of notable contemporaries, and he won the affection of Masons generally by his unsparing exertions in the glorious cause of charity, and in promoting concord and unanimity, brotherly love, morality, and good fellowship, with the strictest order and decorum.

On the death of Dunckerley John Knight, the Provincial Grand Master of Knights Templar in Cornwall, said he had gone into the grave full of years and full of honours 'yet we cannot but deplore that he was taken from us so soon'.

George Downing, who succeeded Dunckerley as Provincial Grand Master of Essex, gave an insight into the man and the Mason in his tribute.

He stood unrivalled for conviviality of disposition, correctness of principles, extent of Masonic knowledge and readiness of communication.

He loved Masonry from his soul, and as his attachment was not the effect of a hasty impression upon a lively imagination, but the result of a long and well-directed scrutiny into the nature and utility of the institution, he seldom failed to communicate a portion of his zeal to those to whom he conversed. In this country he may be considered to have been the father of the Craft . . .'

38

THE DECLINING YEARS

As HE APPROACHED the age of 70 the hardships endured in the Navy and the lack of vitamin C in the diet began to take their toll and Dunckerley suffered a great deal of pain 'with the gout', a term which applied in those days not only to arthritic but also to other unknown complaints.

As early as January 1792 Dunckerley admitted that his health was 'much impaired' and asked that lodge registration fees, lists of members and contributions to the charity be sent direct to the Grand Secretary.

On 20 November 1793 Thomas Bronson wrote that his 'master' was in great pain with the gout in both feet and for the first three months of 1794 he was 'laid up' at Bath. In the May he made his last attendance at Grand Lodge.

Yet, in this very year, this brave but prematurely aged warrior displayed his old defiant spirit when he wrote that if the threatened invasion of the British Isles materialised he would offer his services to the Navy or the Army.

By the spring of 1795 his good friend and loyal Deputy Grand Master of the Knights Templar, William Hannam, wrote of him: '. . . his age and infirmities render him very feeble, but he is in good spirits . . .'. Some idea of the health of Dunckerley is gained from the sentence that 'he did me the honour of eating a bit of fish at my table yesterday . . .' It conjures up a mental picture of an erstwhile hearty man toying with his food.

In the April of 1795 Dunckerley and his wife left Hampton Court for their Portsmouth home and it was from here that he wrote in an unsteady hand a letter which expressed sentiments so out of character that it left little doubt that the pain with which he was afflicted was also clouding his judgment.

During his illness his wife and Captain Hannam had dealt with current masonic business which included a request by Bro John Knight for a dispensation to form a Royal Arch Chapter.

Mrs Dunckerley wrote: '. . . Mr. Dunckerley (who is very ill and unable to write) desires you will apply to Capt. Hannam of the Savoy, London, for the Certificate Sash Crofs &c which will be sent directly. I am Sir, Yours aff^n Sister Ann Dunckerley.'

This letter was never countermanded and it was natural that Knight should continue to write to Hannam, but during a temporary rally Dunckerley became obsessed with the mistaken impression that his authority was being usurped. He wrote the following letter to Knight.

Dear Bro. & Knt, Compn.,

By a letter from Capt. Hannam, I am informed that about 5 weeks ago he recv'd (among other things) from Mr. Knight at Redruth a Petition to the G & R Chapter for a Warrant constituting a Chapter at Truro: but on his application was inform'd that the names were not register'd. If you had apply'd to me, or if Capt. H had apply'd to me, as Superintendant of Cornwall, I should have granted a Dispensation for Truro & the Patent of Confirmation would have been sent to you. This is not the only omifsion that has been found in the Grand Register, owing to hurry & inattention. Whenever Supper was reported to be on the table, the Chapter was immediately clos'd and the loose Papers hurry'd into the drawer of the Desk. On the 22nd June 1973 I re'd your letter dated the 17th. of that month with 17 names to be register'd in Grand Chapter & a Draught for £7 5 6, also 3 names of Knights Compns for which I sent you 3 Certificates. In October 1783, when the G. Chapter met after the summer recefs I sent the 17 names to be registered, and a bank note for £10, part of which (£4 5 0) was on Acct.   your Chapter. I have the letternow before me acknowledging this Receipt. I will have nothing more to do with the G Chapter of R Arch Masons, therefore in future, you will please addrefs Capt Hannam, or any person you please on *that* part of Masonry. But why have you withdrawn your correspondance with me as G Master of the Order of Knts. Templars & apply to Capt H for Certificate? I write in great pain with the Gout in my hand. Believe me Your faithful & affect Bro. &c.

Portsmouth Common: Aug 13, 1795

Dear Bro & Most Comp[n]:

By a letter from Capt Hannam, I am inform'd that about 5 weeks ago, he rec'd (among other things) from Mr Knight at Redruth a Petition to the G & R Chapter for a Warr[an]t to constitute a Chapter at Truro: but on his application was inform'd that the names were not register'd. If You had apply'd to one, or if Capt H had apply'd to one, as Superintendant of Cornwall, I should have granted a Dispensation for & the Patent of Confirmation would have been sent to You. This is not the only omission that has been found in the Grand Register, owing to hurry & inattention. Whenever Supper was reported to be on the Table, the Chapter was immediately clos'd & the loose Papers hurry'd into the drawer of the Desk. On the 22d June 1793 I rec'd your letter dated the 17th of that month with 17 names to be register'd in our G R Chapter & a Draught for £7.5.6, also 3 names of Knights Comp for which I sent you 3 Certificates. In October 1793, when the G Chapter met after the summer recess I sent the 17 names to be register'd, & a bank note for £10, part of which £4.5.6 was on acc of your Chapter. I have the letter now before me acknowledging the Receipt. I will have nothing more to do with the G Chapter of R Arch Masons, therefore in future, You will please to address Capt Hannam, or any person You please on that part of Masonry. But why have you withdrawn your correspondance with me as G Master of the Order of Knts Templars & apply to Capt H for Certificates? I write in great pain with the Gout in my hand. Believe me Your faithful & affect Bro. &c&c Tho Dunckerley

Figure 25
Dunckerley's unpleasant letter to John Knight dated 13 August 1795

The letter was signed 'Thos Dunckerley'.

By courtesy of the Worshipful Master and Librarian of the Cornubian Lodge No 450, Hayle, this letter is reproduced (*Fig* 25). There is also a facsimile of Mrs Dunckerley's letter. It could be the only extant letter written by her. It does establish her Christian name as Ann (*Fig* 26).

Seventeen days after sending his unpleasant letter Dunckerley circularised a printed copy of a letter from Prince Edward to all KT Conclaves. On the one addressed to 'Mr. John Knight, Redruth, Cornwall', he wrote in ink: 'I wrote to Sir John Knight in the course of this month, but have rec'd no answer.'

On 11 September 1795 Knight sent a respectful letter explaining that he had been prevented from making an earlier reply as business had taken him away from home. He added

> My mind has been much grieved at the idea of your supposing me to have entertained a wish to decline corresponding with you. My desire has been always to number you amongst the first of my Masonic friends. I have always read your letters with the greatest satisfaction and (I may add) pride, and I wish I c'd find words to convey to you how much I revere your character as a Mason and a Man. I beg to assure you that you are held in the highest esteem by all your Brethren and Companions in this place.
>
> Having written your letter on the 7th. February last I rec'd an ansr. from Mrs. Dunckerley dated the 19th. of the same month desiring me to apply for the things therein mentioned to Capt. Hannam, which I did, and on the 31st. March I again wrote him on other business, and rec'd his answer dated 4th. April, where-in he stated that you and he had been dining together the preceding day, and that he was to meet you at a Knight Companion's House on that day, when he intended to show you my letter. This is the reason of my addressing him instead of you, and I concluded it met with your entire approbation, and I repeated my correspondence with him under this idea when I applied for a Dispensation for a Chapter at Penryn.
>
> I beg leave once more to express my unfeigned sorrow for having thus involuntarily give you offence. I lament with you the irregularity and inattention with which the Grand Chapter do this business.
>
> I hope the names of All the Companions are now registered, and I request that you will have the goodness to inform yourself of it.

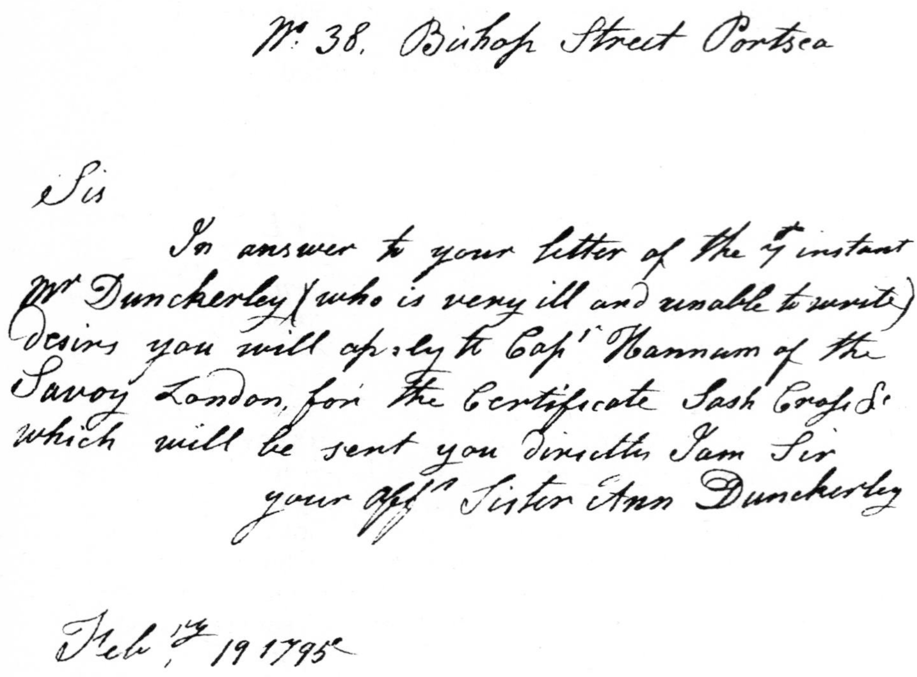

N.º 38. Bishop Street Portsea

Sir
          In answer to your letter of the 5 instant
Mr Dunckerley (who is very ill and unable to write)
desires you will apply to Cap.ᵗ Hannum of the
Savoy London, for the Certificate Sash Cross &.ᶜ
which will be sent you directly I am Sir
                    your Aff.ᵗ Sister Ann Dunckerley

Feb.ʳʸ 19 1795

Figure 26
This could well be the only surviving letter written by Dunckerley's wife
which establishes her Christian name as Ann

My Brethren and Knights Companions in this place desire to unite with me in every sentiment of respect to you and in wishing you success in all your public and private undertakings, and good health and long life in this world and happiness hereafter in the next.

Two months later Thomas Dunckerley was called to receive that 'happiness'.

THE UNMARKED GRAVE

*In a grave, unmarked and now unknown, one
of the great architects of modern Freemasonry
was laid to rest on 27 November 1795.*

Thomas Dunckerley died in a house which was then No 38, Bishop Street, Common, Portsmouth, eight days before. He was interred in the grounds of the Parish Church for Portsea, St Mary's, Kingston. At the end of the last century the church was rebuilt, the tombstones disturbed and some not replaced.

His resting place is far from 'the Temple Church near the Knights Templars' he so admired. But Thomas Dunckerley lies in the county where he first saw the light of Freemasonry and over which he first presided as a Provincial Grand Master.

The lonely grave is marked neither by a stone bearing his name nor the square and compasses, yet there are in England and Wales alone over 7,000 memorials to this great Mason. They are the lodges ranged under the banner of the United Grand Lodge.

And wherever they meet on the face of this earth Freemasons must remember and revere

The Incredible Brother Thomas Dunckerley.

Appendix A

SOME PEOPLE IN THE STORY

THIS APPENDIX IS to give additional information about some of the people who were associated with Dunckerley and his mother and by choice LADY WALPOLE comes first. She was a friend when Mary Dunckerley most needed one.

She arranged the marriage to Mr Dunckerley and in so doing possibly risked royal disfavour.

She was the wife of ROBERT WALPOLE (1676 to 1745), who was a prominent Whig statesman remembered in history as the first English prime minister. He was knighted in 1724 and in 1742 was created Earl of Orford.

Of him it has been said that in an age of venality and lax morals he was the least corrupted, the soberest and the hardest working of the leaders of both factions.

For authentic details of the character of Lady Walpole one can visit Westminster Abbey where there is a life-size statue erected by her youngest son.

A moving tribute on the monument tells us that she had beauty and wit without vice or vanity and cultivated the arts without affectation. She was devout though without bigotry to any sect and was without prejudice to any party 'tho' the wife of a Minifter whose power she esteemed but when She cou'd employ it to benefit the miferable or to reward the meritorious'.

She loved a private life, we are told, though born to shine in public, and was an ornament to courts, untainted by them. She died on 20 August 1737.

SIR EDWARD WALPOLE was the second son of the great Sir Robert. He was born in 1706, knighted in 1753 and died unmarried in 1784. He was secretary to the 3rd Duke of Devonshire. when Lord Lieutenant of Ireland from 1768. His brother ROBERT was auditor of the Exchequer in 1739.

The Prince of Wales who became GEORGE II was born 1783 and died in 1760. He married Caroline of Ansbach and they were crowned at Westminster Abbey on 11 October 1727 and in spite of wars and unrest their reign of 33 years saw the extension of the Empire in India and North America as well as other prosperous periods. In the 1720s they lived at Ormonde Lodge on the Richmond Estate by the river between Richmond and Kew and it was somewhat ironical that it was suggested that Mary Dunckerley should go to Richmond for the birth of her baby.

George II was the last reigning monarch to command his army on the battlefield. This was at Dettingen in 1743 when the French were defeated. A son was wounded in the battle.

Neither George II nor his grandson George III joined the Craft. Two sons of the former are said to have enrolled under the Antients' Banner. Three of the five brothers of George III were members as also were six of his sons.

Another person who befriended Mary in her time of great need was LADY RANELAGH, the second wife of the much older EARL OF RANELAGH who held several government appointments and had the unenviable distinction of being convicted in February 1702 of misappropriation of £72,000 as Paymaster General and being expelled from the House of Commons.

Before her marriage she was Margaret, Dowager Baroness Stawell and the fourth daughter of the Earl of Salisbury. She died in 1728 aged 54 and was buried at Chiswick. Her husband predeceased her by 16 years dying with 'neither place nor pension . . . and a great many debts'.

What Lady Ranelagh's position was in court circles is not known but possibly she found favour. Ailesbury's Memoirs (vol ii, p 447) refers to her as a 'beautiful widow' but, at the most, with the wherewithal only to live comfortably.

Ranelagh House was to the east of Chelsea Hospital but it was demolished early in the nineteenth century.

LADY RANELAGH and LADY STANLEY were London neighbours and Mary's condition was undoubtedly the subject of gossip between them.

Philip Dormer Stanhope, the 4th EARL OF CHESTERFIELD, was

born 1694 and died 1773. He was Lord of the Bed Chamber from 1715 to 1730. He married in 1733 the illegitimate daughter of George I. Thomas Dunckerley was therefore her natural step-nephew – if such a relationship is recognised! Lord Chesterfield was made a freemason in Grand Lodge on 24 June 1721 when he was 27 years of age. He maintained his interest in the Craft and in 1731 when he was Lord Ambassador at the Hague he assisted at the initiation of His Royal Highness, Francis Duke of Lorrain.

Prince William Henry, DUKE OF CLARENCE, the third son of George III, was crowned William IV in 1830 and reigned for seven years. He was initiated in the Pope's Head Tavern, which was then meeting in Foxhole (Vauxhall) Street, Plymouth, on 9 March 1786, and Grand Lodge, in recognition of the honour conferred on the Society, presented him with an apron lined with blue silk and gave him the rank of Past Grand Master.

Prince William was Master of the Prince of Wales Lodge from 1827 to 1830 and Patron of the Grand Chapter of the Royal Arch for many years in honour of which a medal was struck. The Lodge in which he was initiated was erased in 1828.

At the time of his initiation he was serving in the Royal Navy. Some 40 years later he visited Plymouth as Lord High Admiral of England and the local freemasons prepared an address for presentation to their royal brother. Prince William addressed his acknowledgement to 'Gentlemen and Brother Masons' and in it he recalled being 'received a Mason' in Plymouth.

His brother PRINCE EDWARD, the fourth son of King George III, was born on 2 November 1767 and his rigorous training for a military career began when he was sent to Germany at the age of 18. In 1787 his father sent him to Geneva where he spent three happy years and was initiated in the Lodge l'Union on 5 August 1789 at the age of 22. When this was announced in the Grand Lodge in England it was decided to present him with an apron and also give him the rank of Past Grand Master.

When he left Geneva the following year he took with him the good wishes of the Lodge members who expressed regret at the departure of 'a real brother', who had served their lodge as Junior Warden.

The Prince was immediately sent for instruction in garrison duties to Gibraltar and he was immediately appointed by warrant Provincial Grand Master for the Garrison, Town and Territory of Gibraltar and held the office for 10 years, under the 'Moderns'.

In 1791 he went to Quebec with the 7th Royal Fusiliers and there he found the social life compensated for the 'Savage climate' and he became the Provincial Grand Master of Lower Canada under the 'Antients' and was instrumental in the setting up of a coalition of the rival Grand Lodges which helped the eventual formation of the United Grand Lodge in 1813.

Prince Edward was a strict disciplinarian but it is on record that in Lodge he once corrected a member who referred to him as His Royal Highness by saying that 'here we are all brethren'. He continued as Provincial Grand Master after his return to England.

In January 1794 he left Quebec for Martinique to take part in the campaign against the French West India Islands and served with gallantry. On 10 May 1794 he arrived at Halifax and spent four years to November 1798 in Nova Scotia.

He was created Duke of Kent and Strathearn in 1799 and was appointed Commander-in-Chief of troops in North America but continued to be masonically active and attended Grand Lodge meetings.

In 1802 he was back in Gibraltar for a year's stay as Governor and then to England where he was actively associated with Masonic charities, and became Patron of the Knights Templar.

On 8 November 1813 he was elected Grand Master of the 'Antients' and when on 27 December United Grand Lodge assembled for its inaugural meeting he proposed his brother the Duke of Sussex as Grand Master.

In 1819 the Duke of Kent and Strathearn, his wife and their baby daughter went to live at Sidmouth in Devonshire where he died suddenly on 23 January 1820. His daughter became Queen Victoria.

Like Dunckerley CAPTAIN MARK ROBINSON entered the Navy as a boy, aged 14, and rose to the rank of Rear Admiral. He frequently distinguished himself in the service of his country. As commander of HMS *Falcon* his conduct and bravery were conspicuous at the reduction of Gaudaloupe where his ship sank under him. As Commander of the *Shrewsbury* he led the British Fleet five times into action and in the last of these engagements off Cape Virginia he was severely wounded which resulted in the loss of a leg.

Robinson was initiated in 1747 and became the 'father' of the Lodge of Antiquity. He died at his house in Henrietta Street, Bath, on 23 November 1799, four years after Dunckerley who had served under him in HMS *Vanguard*.

Robinson was one of the earliest friends of the immortal Admiral Lord Nelson.

JOHN KNIGHT of Redruth who was Dunckerley's loyal friend was initiated in the Druids Lodge on 31 December 1766 and became one of the most active and well-informed freemasons of his day. He was exalted in the Chapter of Sincerity at the Peace and Fame Inn, Plymouth Dock (Devonport) in 1775 and was installed a Knight Templar on 29 April 1777 and he rendered outstanding service. By occupation he was a mercer. He died in 1828/9 aged 82.

CHEVALIER BARTHOLOMEW RUSPINI was born in Northern Italy in 1728. He studied surgery at the hospital in Bergamo and then placed himself under the tuition of the dentist to the King of France. He came to England in 1750 and was accepted in social and professional spheres and became the dentist to King George III.

He was initiated in Bush Lodge No 116 in Bristol in 1762 and became associated with several lodges. He was Grand Steward in 1772 and then promoted Grand Sword Bearer in 1792 until such time as he desired to resign the office. A wonderful honour well earned! He was also active in the Royal Arch Degree.

His name, however, will for ever be linked with the Royal Masonic Institution for Girls. Ruspini was the first treasurer of the Institution and a life member of all the committees. After his death in 1813 two of his grandchildren were educated at the school.

LORD DIGBY by whose interest Dunckerley was superannuated from the Navy was Baron Digby of Gedshill, Lord of the

Admiralty from 1763 to 1765 and MP for Wiltshire 1761–5.

RICHARD WORSLEY succeeded to the baronetcy in 1768 on the death of his father Thomas. He was MP for Newport, Isle of Wight and of Newtown and also served as Governor of the Island. He was Controller of the Royal Household.

Captain the Hon JOHN RUTHVEN was the second son of James, third Lord Ruthven. He was initiated at the age of 23 in the Royal Navy Lodge, Deal, on 7 September 1762. He was then Captain of the *Terpsichore* frigate which was taken from the French in 1760.

Appendix B

AN IMPORTANT MANUSCRIPT

THE GRAND LODGE No 1 Manuscript, the first to be deposited in the Library and Museum at United Grand Lodge in London was bought in 1839 from a Miss Siddall for £25.

The description of her by R. F. Gould 'an elderly spinster grand daughter of the second wife' of Dunckerley is inaccurate.

Dunckerley was married when he was only 20 and had been married for 50 years when he died at the end of 1795, predeceasing his wife by over five years.

There were two spinster sisters by the name of Siddall; Ann, who lived at Hampton Court and Susannah of Plymouth. They were described by Dunckerley as 'much loved friends' who extended affectionate regard and attention to him and his wife and in appreciation of this he willed that after his wife's decease his household goods and other furniture should be shared equally between the two sisters. This could account for the manuscript coming into the possession of one of the Misses Siddall.

The Manuscript is a parchment about 5 inches wide and 9 feet long and is dated 25 December 1583.

The question which remains is how did the manuscript come into Dunckerley's possession. Did he realise its importance and significance? If he had, he would surely have mentioned it in his Will.

Bibliography: Sources Consulted

College of Arms
Complete Peerage
Coombe Library: Cornubian Lodge No 450, Hayle
Dictionaries of biography (various)
Dunckerley – numerous people of that name
Exmouth Library
Grand Lodge Library, Freemasons' Hall, London
Gentlemans' Magazine
History of P.G.L. of Hampshire & the I.O.W., 1832–1932, compiled by W Bro W. J. Finemore
History of Freemasonry, R. F. Gould
History of Freemasonry in Wiltshire, F. H. Goldney (1880)
History of Provincial Grand Lodge of Essex, K. S. Buck
History of Lodge of Fortitude No 105, S. J. Bradford (1959)
History of Freemasonry in West Cornwall 1765–1828, Osborn
History of Mark Master Masons in Province of Devonshire, Ron Chudley (1980)
Honourable Society of the Inner Temple
Hughan's Roll of Lodges
George Norman Masonic Museum and Library, Bath
John Lane Memorial Library: Jordan Lodge No 1402
Freemasons' – Magazine; *Freemasons' Quarterly*; *Freemasons' Pocket Companion*, Smith (1738)
Freemasonry in Bristol, Powell and Littleton
Grand Lodge History, Calvert
Library and Museum, PGL Worcestershire
Maritime Library, Plymouth
Ministry of Defence Library
Masonic Songs (1885)
National Army Museum
National Maritime Museum, Greenwich

Provincial G Lodges of – Bristol, Cornwall, Devonshire, Dorset, Essex, Gloucester, Herefordshire, Somerset, Gibraltar (DGL)

Provincial Grand Lodge of Essex 1776–1976, K. S. Buck

Plymouth Polytechnic (Dept, Marine Science)

Quatuor Coronati Lodge No 2076 transactions

Royal Archives, Windsor Castle

Royal Hampshire Regiment archives

Royal College of Physicians

Record Office, Kew

Trustees of the Chatsworth Settlement (Devonshire collection)

Thomas Dunckerley, Henry Sadler (1891)

Westminster Abbey

And numerous brethren and lodges to whom thanks extended.

Index

Page numbers in *italic* refer to illustrations or their captions; *passim* denotes that there are references scattered throughout the pages referred to; *bis* denotes that there is more than one reference on the page.

Lodges are all English Constitution unless otherwise indicated. An asterisk * indicates that the lodge has been erased or the number pre-dates the last closing up of lodge numbers in 1963.